THE DRAMATIC CRITICISM OF

GEORGE JEAN NATHAN

THE DRAMATIC CRITICISM OF

George Jean Nathan

BY CONSTANCE FRICK

INTER FOLIA
FRUCTUS

ITHACA · NEW YORK

CORNELL UNIVERSITY PRESS · 1943

Cornell University Press

Foreign Agent:

LONDON: Humphrey Milford

Oxford University Press

PRINTED IN THE UNITED STATES OF AMERICA

Designed by Robert Josephy

Foreword by George Jean Nathan

I HAVE BEEN ASKED to contribute a brief foreword to this treatise on my art and morals and, while politely complying, I frankly do not know just how to go about it. I might very well write, as subjects invariably do under such circumstances, that I am flattered that anyone should devote his efforts to thus solidifying me in the quicksands of posterity. I might also very well write, as is further the custom, that while I disagree with some of the author's conclusions I am not certain that my disagreement means that she is wrong and that I am correct. I might in turn write that while I concur heartily in the author's intermittent esteem for my critical talents, I am not certain that my rapt concurrence may not indicate a deplorable critical astigmatism on my part. Or still again I might confect a foreword gratuitously rich in quotations from Brunetière, Sainte-Beuve, Coleridge, Hazlitt and, satirically, the drama critics of the present-day tonier weeklies and monthlies, thus testifying to my liberal library education and boring the reader, who is seldom deceived by such extrinsic shenanigan, no end.

v

I might, as I say, do some or all of this, but tactfully I for the most part refrain. I have read Miss Frick's study of my modest efforts to assist in making the American theatre and its drama worthier of the attention of quality audiences, and I tell only the simple personal truth when I set down my opinion that she has done, in the main, a painstaking, intelligent, shrewd, and generally capital job. Her patience in plowing through the mass of my critical writings astounds me, since I myself have little such patience in any direction. Her gift of selection seems to me to be skilful and pointed, and her summary of my critical ideas, particularly since they have been occasionally and superficially contradictory, is clear-headed and clear-stated.

One who, like myself, has written millions upon millions of words in the long service of his craft can at best be a feeble judge of the current merit of what at least a third of them have endeavored to express; the profuse flow sends up a spray that confuses the vision. Miss Frick has penetrated that spray and has filtered from the blinding cataract, deftly and sagaciously, the drops which appear to her to possess some virtue. I congratulate myself that so expert a manipulator of the sieve has been willing to apply herself to the heroic task.

Preface

THIS BOOK is the result of a study of the critical principles of George Jean Nathan. In justification of
the study, I submit Nathan's importance as a critic; the
fact that his theories of drama and standards of criticism,
scattered as they are through the miscellany of twenty-
odd volumes, warrant and require winnowing, a task
which he himself probably never would undertake; and,
finally, the unavailability of two earlier and faintly similar
treatises. Goldberg's *The Theatre of George Jean Nathan*, published in 1926, is now out of print. Since its
publication, furthermore, Nathan has added eleven volumes to his critical works. And Vladimar Kozlenko's *The
Quintessence of Nathanism*, published in a limited edi-
tion of three hundred copies in 1930, has been out of
print since 1931.

My treatment differs from the two previous studies in
that it is wholly objective. I have analyzed, not criticized,
Nathan's criticism, attempting to give the gist and eliminate the trivia without sacrificing his literary grace. Various contradictions and Nathan's occasional buffoonery

in sober garb have complicated the task, not to mention the mental hazard provided by his statement that not one in a hundred of his readers really understands accurately what he is trying to say.

It is not often that a living person is the subject of a study such as this. Among the disadvantages is the fact that any résumé is necessarily incomplete, for the work is going on, opinions are being altered, achievements are piling up. Among the advantages, however—and there are many—one looms large: the fact that the man himself, if he sees fit to do so, can answer questions of importance.

A few months ago I wrote to Nathan, asking him this question: "Excluding your encouragement of O'Neill, what do you consider your greatest contribution as a critic to American drama, the theatre, or dramatic criticism?"

Nathan very generously found time to reply, listing his contributions as follows: "The introduction into the American theatre of the best of the modern European dramatists; the encouragement of young native playwrights like Saroyan, et al.; the gesture toward a reformation of the general critical attitude toward the theatre and drama."

It has been my task to draw together under significant headings and in compact form the principles and methods of the work to which Nathan has devoted many years.

PREFACE

I wish to express my sincerest gratitude to those who have assisted me: to Dr. Stith Thompson for his ready advice and reasoned judgment; to Miss Ruth Leeson, reference librarian of the Fort Wayne Public Library, for supplying information on the Nirdlinger family in the early days of Fort Wayne; and to Mr. Nathan himself for graciously answering those questions which I considered sufficiently important to warrant his attention.

Constance Frick

Evansville, Indiana
July 15, 1942

CONTENTS

THE DRAMATIC CRITICISM OF

GEORGE JEAN NATHAN

CHAPTER ONE

Nathan's Life and Works

"TELL me what a dramatic critic eats and drinks, how far north of Ninetieth Street he lives, what he considers a pleasant evening when he is not in the theatre, and what kind of lingerie his wife wears," Nathan challenges us, "and I'll tell you with very few misses what kind of critic he is. I'll tell you whether he is fit to appreciate Schnitzler, or whether he is fit only for Augustus Thomas. . . . The criticism is the man; the man the criticism." [1]

George Jean Nathan lives forty-six blocks south of Ninetieth Street—without a wife; drinks with a fastidious thirst; and enjoys delicate femininity on his rare night off. But if you think that he is fit only for Augustus Thomas, you are mistaken. Nathan is the man who exploded the great Thomas myth. And that alone entitles him to a somewhat more detailed biographical treatment.

[1] Nathan, George Jean, *The Critic and the Drama* (New York, 1922), pp. 118–19. In the footnotes Nathan's works hereafter will be referred to without the author's name.

It is hard to believe that the cosmopolite in an habitual top hat and with forty-eight overcoats in his wardrobe came out of Indiana. Came out, indeed. He left at the age of six and has never been back. But the roots of the Nathan and Nirdlinger families are deep in the Hoosier soil, and the traits of his Fort Wayne ancestors live again in his books.

Precursor of his pioneering criticism is his pioneering grandfather, guiding a covered wagon to a far outpost in Indiana. Only one wagon road to the West had been broken when Frederic Nirdlinger, a young German-American, brought his wife by covered wagon from Chambersburg, Pennsylvania, to Fort Wayne, at that time an Indian fort without a single house. Nirdlinger, then a cattleman and frontier trader, was one of the first three settlers at Fort Wayne, and later helped to build it up as a mid-Western trading-post. But no pioneer's log cabin was to be the future home of Frederic.[2] That home was to be an impressive square brick house with a wide lawn surrounded by ornate fences of iron foliage: one of the show places of early Fort Wayne. In this home, in 1882, George Jean Nathan was born.

Nathan's mother was Ella Nirdlinger, one of eight children. His father was Charles Narét-Nathan, a native of Lorraine and the son of a leading Parisian criminal

[2] Griswold, Bert J., *The Pictorial History of Fort Wayne, Indiana* (Chicago, 1917).

lawyer. The cosmopolitanism of the father surpassed even that of his son. Charles Narét-Nathan was graduated from Heidelberg; owned vineyards in France and coffee plantations in Brazil; spoke eight languages; had lived six years in Argentina, eight years in Brazil, two years in India, and three in China. The *Wanderlust* had carried him around the world, but it was the metropolises—not the hinterlands—that interested him, just as they interest his son. "The country," George Jean once said, "is for yokels and cows. . . . I have not been back to Fort Wayne in twenty-five years and I'll probably never go back. Ditto, Cleveland. My future is in New York—and London, Paris and Rome." [3]

When George Jean was six, the family moved from Fort Wayne to Cleveland. Here George was tutored privately and read omnivorously, particularly history and plays. He also attended school in Cleveland and spent alternate summers in Europe. In 1898, he studied in Paris; in 1900, he studied the graphic arts in Bologna, Naples, Venice, and Rome; in the summer of 1902—this time in company with his father—he learned more languages at Heidelberg.

Four years at Cornell University followed. "I went to Cornell," Nathan says, "because all the boys from Cleveland were going to Cornell that year." Here he quickly displayed an interest in dramatics and journalism and

[3] Goldberg, *The Theatre of George Jean Nathan* (1926), p. 46.

3

in didoes akin to those which later distinguished the
Mencken-Nathan *Smart Set* period. He helped to write
skits for the Savage Club's annual shows and once played
—in a long, taffy-blond wig—a French hussy to a chorus
line composed largely of the football team in skirts! He
served as an editor of *The Widow* and also of the *Cornell
Daily Sun*. As chairman of the Cornell Spring Day, he
was responsible for the creation of the mysterious
"Mzupzi," a campus sensation for antecedent weeks
which ultimately was revealed—at a quarter a head—to
be the two-year-old son of the colored cook at the Cayuga
Hotel. "Those were serious days," says Nathan. He also
was chairman of the *Widow* Ball, the first which the
Cornell Widow ever put on, a roughhouse never equalled
at the University which lasted from ten o'clock one Fri-
day night until eight A. M. the following Tuesday and
landed no less than fifty participants in the Cornell in-
firmary. "But there was a nurse there," Nathan recalls,
"who was so beautiful that the boys would frequently and
deliberately sprain ankles in order to be ministered to by
her. I recall four sprained ankles of my own, to say nothing of three sprained wrists and a hypothetical terrible
case of cramps." Nathan received his A. B. from Cornell
in 1904, and a year at the University of Bologna in Italy
completed his "formal" education.

The effects of this training and of his home background

4

are obvious. Sophistication is the almost inevitable result of a youth spent in such surroundings. Nathan's independence of mind, his utter disregard for the opinions of others when he expresses his own opinions, his general air of aloofness may be attributed, at least in part, to the private tutoring. The "strange overtones of democracy" in his aristocracy date, perhaps, from his days in the Cleveland school. "In every thoroughly charming and effective person one finds a suggestion and trace, however small, of the gutter." And there can be no doubt that George Jean Nathan is a thoroughly charming and effective person—by his own definition the most delightful of companions, "he who combines the mind of a gentleman with the emotions of a bum." [4]

He is a strange blend, a perpetual paradox, at once a clashing and a harmonizing of the strains he bears. He is the thorough German scholar, his profound learning masked by his Gallic wit and his Gallic-American practicality. Most surprising in an American critic, he is, like his father, the complete cosmopolite, thoroughly familiar with the drama and the theatre of every land, however distant or insignificant.

Grandfather Frederic, heading his covered wagon down the wilderness trail, displayed no greater zest than Nathan pioneering in aesthetic fields.

[4] *The Autobiography of an Attitude*, p. 50.

The family influence had never made itself more strongly felt—or more beneficently—than the day George Jean stood upon the threshold of his first job. Uncle Charles Frederic Nirdlinger was a close friend and former editorial associate of James Gordon Bennett, owner of the *New York Herald*, and Uncle S. F. Nixon had given a great deal of early assistance to William C. Reick, Bennett's chief lieutenant and executive editor of the paper. As a result, young George became a cub reporter on that newspaper at the staggering salary of $15 a week. "And no matter how many stories I covered or how well the work went, they wouldn't raise me above $15 a week," he added later. He covered special assignments, murder trials, sports events—often with more fancy than fact—before being promoted into the Sunday department. His two stories a week in this capacity left ample time for ventures into the field of dramatic criticism. As third-string reviewer for the *Herald*, he covered unimportant plays, fretting the while under the policy of the paper which always gave first and tender consideration to its big advertisers.

Nathan's interest in dramatic criticism was of long standing. He had been a student of drama and the stage for years. Here, too, he felt the influence of his uncles. Charles Frederic Nirdlinger was a celebrated drama critic and playwright; S. F. Nixon was an important theatrical figure in Philadelphia and the nation and was one of the

6

founders of the famous theatrical firm of Nixon and Zimmerman; and Frank Nixon was general manager of the five Nixon theatres in Philadelphia. It is only natural that Nathan found his way into the dramatic field—only natural, too, that a man of his upbringing and temperament did not long endure the intellectual servility demanded of him on the *Herald*.

His opportunity came sooner than he expected. In 1906, as he was walking down the street one day considering the *Herald's* offer to transfer him to their London staff—still at $15 a week—he met another former editor of the *Cornell Daily Sun*, Lynn G. Wright, editor of *Outing* and *The Bohemian* magazines. On the spot, Wright offered Nathan the dramatic editorship of both periodicals. And Nathan accepted. "You walk down a certain street at a certain time and meet a man, and there you are!"

A long series of magazine associations followed. In 1908, Nathan joined the staff of *Harper's Weekly*, writing primarily on the stage and the drama. In the same year, he began his association with the *Smart Set*, serving as dramatic critic until 1923 and as co-editor, with H. L. Mencken, from 1914 to 1923. In addition, he has over the years written the dramatic criticism for *Puck, Judge,* the New York Sunday *Telegraph* and McClure Syndicates, for *The New Freeman, Scribner's, The Saturday Review of Literature, Life, Vanity Fair, Newsweek,* and

Esquire. He has served as consulting editor of *Arts & Decoration;* as co-founder, co-editor and co-critic, with Mencken, of *The American Mercury;* as co-founder, co-editor and critic of *The American Spectator;* and has contributed criticism to such an assortment as the London *Daily Express,* the London *Sunday Chronicle, Cosmopolitan, Liberty, Current History, Der Querschnitt, Die Literatur, Die Neue Rundschau* and *Mercure de France,* as well as to Dutch and Italian periodicals, and regularly to the *Encyclopaedia Britannica* and the *Britannica Book of the Year.*

Today he has the reputation of being the highest paid dramatic critic of any time or any country, and is one of the very few American critics who ever have attained international prestige.

When Nathan was called to join the staff of the *Smart Set,* he found there one H. L. Mencken, engaged the month before to review books. Nathan was only twenty-six, Mencken twenty-eight, but the intellectual association thus begun has wielded, in its way, an influence on American literature and drama unsurpassed in the history of this country. The work which Mencken and Nathan began as *Smart Set* literary and dramatic critic, respectively, they continued as co-editors. St. John Ervine, viewing the situation from London, put his finger on the nature of that influence:

8

I doubt if any persons in America have done more than these two to prevent Americans from allowing their enthusiasms to run away with their intelligence. Steadfastly judging American work by the highest standards, they have helped to raise American work to the level of the highest standards. The fact that a rich and vigorous literature is now pouring out of the United States is due in large measure to Mr. Mencken and Mr. Nathan.[5]

The *Smart Set* discovered, among others, Eugene O'Neill and F. Scott Fitzgerald. It introduced or fostered many writers at that time comparative unknowns in this country, among them Lord Dunsany, Theodore Dreiser as a poet and playwright, James Branch Cabell as a playwright, James Joyce, Aldous Huxley, Anatole France, Frank Norris, Stephen Crane, Ruth Suckow, Jim Tully, James Stephens, and dozens upon dozens of others. It attacked with gusto and Rabelaisian humor many of the reigning American dramatists and producers—let the chips fall where they might—and demanded a new and higher set of critical standards.

Naturally, this pioneering roused a storm of opposition. William Saroyan accused Mencken and Nathan of trying to please an audience:

[5] Ervine, St. John, "Ervine on Nathan," *The Living Age*, CCCXL (May, 1931), 306.

9

And it must be a most singularly uncivilized audience, composed mostly of the type of people who find it highly gratifying to assume they belong to the sophisticated minority and who suppose themselves not to be Babbitts. They are the ones who want to be among the few with sense enough to laugh at things.[6]

Much of the opposition, however, took the form of pleasantries, of which Berton Braley's "Three—Minus One" is the most widely known.

There were three that sailed away one night
Away from the madding throng;
And two of the three were always right
And every one else was wrong.
But they took another along, these two,
To bear them company,
For he was the only One ever knew
Why the other two should be;
And so they sailed away, these three—
Mencken,
Nathan
And God.

[6] Saroyan, William, "The American Clowns of Criticism," *Overland Monthly*, LXXXVII (March, 1929), 77. Saroyan was twenty years old when he wrote this article attacking Mencken and Nathan.

And the two they talked of the aims of Art,
    Which they alone understood;
And they quite agreed from the very start
    That nothing was any good
Except some novels that Dreiser wrote
    And some plays from Germany.
When God objected—they rocked the boat
    And dropped him into the sea,
'For you have no critical facultee,'
        Said Mencken
        And Nathan
        To God.

The two come cheerfully sailing home
    Over the surging tide
And trod once more on their native loam,
    Wholly self-satisfied;
And the little group that calls them great
    Welcomed them fawningly.
Though why the rest of us tolerate
    This precious pair must be
Something nobody else can see
        But Mencken,
        Nathan
        And God!

The *enfants terribles* answered these pleasantries by pub-
licly announcing their candidacy for president and vice-

president of the United States. They published in the pages of the magazine their platform of one hundred and twenty-two planks, including the now celebrated promise that, if elected, they would shave off the whiskers of Charles Evans Hughes.

Meanwhile, standing like two enormous toads in the swank offices of the *Smart Set* were a couple of large tin spittoons, symbolizing the deliberate heresies of the two critics. Mencken and Nathan assured their partners and publishers, whose delicate sensibilities were highly offended, that the spittoons could be covered with chintz when poets entered the office.

But the two men were, after these many years, slowly drifting apart. As subsequent founders and co-editors of *The American Mercury*, they discovered their interests gradually growing more and more widely separated. The arts alone concerned Nathan; Mencken was interested in politics, economics, and the like. And so, after more than twenty years' association, they parted. But they remain firm and admiring friends who still drink together, juleps preferred.

"What interests me in life . . . is the surface of life: life's music and color, its charm and ease, its humor and its loveliness," Nathan confesses in the foreword to *The World in Falseface*.

In other words, Nathan is a man who believes that the

highest happiness in life comes from doing one's job thoroughly well; from avoiding indignation, irritation, and homely women; and from letting the uplift go hang. No professional reformer, no shepherd to the great American public, he prides himself on his selfishness and his indifference. The philosophy of indifference he considers the greatest of all secrets to human happiness. "I was born indifferent, and at forty I find myself unchanged in attitude. Indignation does not make, and never has made, the world any better than has my own objectionable philosophy of contentful *laissez faire*." [7] As for selfishness, he says, "I doubt, indeed, if there ever has lived an intelligent man whose end in life was not the achievement of a large and selfish pleasure." [8] All art is hedonistic; every true artist is a profound hedonist; and so, too, is George Jean Nathan.

For these confessions and others similar, Nathan frequently has been termed a poseur and an attitudinizer by those who fail to realize that he is completely a man of the theatre, that his "still, sunlit, cozy library" is a stage set, even as the stage is his library and his world. The most diverting and not the least important of all the productions of the American theatre, Randolph Bartlett calls him. "Only the ocular proof of his existence refutes the suspicion that he was invented by the theatre managers

[7] *The World in Falseface*, p. xxii.
[8] *The Autobiography of an Attitude*, p. 6.

13

to make their activities seem worthy of intelligent consideration." [9]

The ocular proof is a slim, dark fellow of middle height, a dandy and a man-about-town, the Beau Brummel of his profession. Fifteen years or so ago his eternally youthful appearance had become almost legendary, as frequently described across the country as his hypochondriac delusions and his extensive wardrobe. Today, graying and handsome, he continues to maintain his rather luxurious though "somewhat fusty" bachelor apartment in West Forty-fourth Street. On every table and every chair, books are stacked seven feet high, and here and there are visible cases of wines and liquors. In this atmosphere of mellow well-being he spends his mornings reading, his afternoons writing. Dinner parties he detests; clubs bore him; callers, social or business, are intruders. When evening comes, there is left, he agrees with Goethe, the theatre.

"I sometimes wonder," Mencken once wrote, "what keeps such a man in the theatre, breathing bad air nightly, gaping at prancing imbeciles, sitting cheek by jowl with cads." [10] Nathan himself supplies the answer. Neither enthusiasm, to which he claims to be constitutionally opposed, nor curiosity, though it is habitual with

[9] Bartlett, Randolph, "Exterminator of Humbugs," *The Saturday Review of Literature*, XI (Jan. 12, 1935), 419.

[10] Mencken, H. L., *Prejudices: First Series* (New York, 1919), p. 216.

him, explains his devotion to the theatre. It is to Mencken's final indictment—"a secret romanticism—a lingering residuum of a boyish delight in pasteboard and spangles, gaudy colors and soothing sounds, preposterous heroes and appetizing wenches"—that Nathan pleads guilty. The theatre, to Nathan, is a great toy, and so it is that he writes of it.

The joys of the world—art, beauty, and "the aesthetic happiness of the minority"—interest Nathan. And in the degree to which it can supply them, the theatre interests him. Meanwhile, its grab-bag nature lures him in. "It is not curiosity that takes me there, but hope." For one memorable night in the theatre, he declares, "I have gladly and willingly suffered the empyreuma of three hundred crab-apples; for one splendid, beautiful and haunting evening, the gases of three hundred boob machines." [11] Or, applying Nathan's comment on a Pinero drama to the entire theatre, it has its moments, but they are swallowed up in its hours.

Of course, the glad and willing sufferance of three hundred crab-apples is a flagrant exaggeration, as anyone will realize who has seen Mr. Nathan gather up his hat and walking stick and stride out of the theatre twenty-one minutes after the curtain has risen, leaving the producer, his play condemned, close to loud curses. The Nathan patience has definite limitations, and the Nathan exits

[11] *The Theatre, the Drama, the Girls,* p. 65.

are of grave importance, for he has declared that any critic who cannot judge the quality of a play accurately and finally in twenty minutes is a rank incompetent.

Despite his frequent abrupt departures, Nathan is only too glad to linger and enjoy good drama—of any type—for his is the most catholic taste of any living dramatic critic. One of the first to yell for Ziegfeld's *Follies*, he has confessed that he reads Shakespeare and Racine for diversion; likes Al Jolson, Smith and Dale, Brahms and Jerome Kern; venerates Molière and Dorothy McGuire's legs; considers George M. Cohan a more expert playwright than Euripides or Calderon; applauds Sean O'Casey, Steinbeck, Schnitzler, Saroyan, Carroll, Shaw, and Dunsany. But he does not hesitate to condemn them all when condemnation is due. "The critic who cannot enjoy *Hamlet* one night and the *Follies* the next seems to me to have something constitutionally wrong with him," he once observed. "*Shuffle Along* has its place in the theatre, and in criticism perhaps no less, equally with *Connais-toi* and *Heartbreak House*." [12]

Perhaps this catholicity of interest accounts in part for Nathan's vast knowledge of the drama. Twenty-four years ago Gordon Craig wrote that Nathan "knows far more about the theatre than all the honorary pallbearers of criticism rolled together." [13] Today, steeped in the drama

[12] *Materia Critica*, p. 30.
[13] Mencken, *op. cit.*, p. 209.

—both stage and closet—of every country and every period, and with an encyclopedic store of first-hand information on the plays, the players, and the playwrights of the last thirty-five years, Nathan still stands unchallenged in his field.

There is no use, most critics agree, in trying to argue with him. Of course, some people do try. You can see them on the sidewalk in front of the theatre at intermission time, an interested onlooker reports, "—often just before Mr. Nathan, wrapping around him the fur coat he has, they say, taught to growl, goes briskly elsewhere. You can tell those who are arguing with Mr. Nathan because they have their mouths open, look a little dazed, and are obviously out on their feet. Mr. Nathan has, you may be sure, cited the works of three French playwrights, two Germans, and one Bulgarian to prove that, as they uneasily suspected from the first, they do not know what they are talking about. And you may be sure, also, that Mr. Nathan has been gentle with them." [14]

To his background of knowledge and experience, Nathan brings a cool non-partisanship which enables him to say of the theatre: "I do not take it very seriously, for I am of the sort that takes nothing very seriously; nor on the other hand do I take it too lightly . . . I take it simply as, night in and night out, it comes before my

[14] Lockridge, Richard, "The Nathan Phenomenon," *The Saturday Review of Literature*, XXV (Jan. 24, 1942), 12.

eyes: a painted toy with something of true gold inside it." [15]

"Once again each year the theatre hitches up its garters, powders its nose, and saunters forth flirtatiously . . . Once again each year the charwomen brush part of the dust off the plush seats, remove the wads of chewing gum from underneath and make ready the house of Thespis for new customers." [16] And once again each year Alfred A. Knopf prepares to publish another volume of the theatrical observations and opinions of George Jean Nathan.

In the last twenty-seven years Nathan has written twenty-eight books, including three collaborations. Of the twenty-five books by Nathan alone, one is a novel (*Monks Are Monks*), and only one (*The New American Credo*) does not deal wholly or in part with the theatre.

"Everybody knows," as Randolph Bartlett observed, "there is not that much to be said about the theatre that is worth saying." [17] The explanation is that Nathan's twenty-five books of critical miscellany are well padded—delightfully padded, to be sure—but padded, nonetheless, with dramatic, theatrical, philosophical, historical, and miscellaneous amblings. They make no pretense of

[15] *The World in Falseface*, p. xxix.
[16] *The Autobiography of an Attitude*, p. 222.
[17] Bartlett, *loc. cit.*

being anything else, and that is half the secret of their charm. Almost inevitably they are front-heavy. The reader who seeks dramatic theory will find two-thirds of it packed into the first third of the book, but if he lays down the volume at that point he will miss most of the fun. This despite the fact that Nathan's books are often largely a compilation of his magazine articles.

Raucous, brilliant, malicious, shrewd and paradoxical, Nathan's volumes are thoroughly worldly, thoroughly American, and above all, thoroughly readable. For a penetrating comment on his earlier style, we do well to turn to his former collaborator, Mencken, who, in 1919, wrote:

> It would be difficult, in all his books, to find a dozen of the usual rubber stamps of criticism; I daresay it would kill him, or, at all events, bring him down with cholera morbus, to discover that he had called a play "convincing" or found "authority" in the snorting of an English actor-manager. At best, this incessant flight from the obvious makes for a piquant, arresting style, a procession of fantastic and often highly pungent neologisms—in brief, for Nathanism. At worst, it becomes artificiality, obscurity.[18]

[18] Mencken, *op. cit.*, p. 221.

But even in 1919 Nathan was taking on "a sedater habit, both in style and in point of view. Without abandoning anything essential, without making the slightest concession to the orthodox opinion that he so magnificently disdains, he yet begins to yield to the middle years. The mere shocking of the stupid is no longer as charming as it used to be." [19]

Thus, today, although Nathan describes fewer plays as "macaronic vacuity" or "pure rouge-stick walla-walla," which plays have evoked—from other critics, of course —either "bedizened encomiastic adjectives" (a dose of gravy) or "vociferous ululations" (lugubrious flap-doodle) —although, in other words, Nathan's style is less startling and less self-conscious, it is and probably always will be distinctly unorthodox and independent of academic standards, as invigorating as an icy draft.

After thirty-five years of the Nathan formula of linguistic dexterity, raffish mocking, gusty candor, and startling paradoxes, some of Nathan's steady readers begin to show signs of reaching the point of satiation. But the ring-master of American criticism will nonetheless continue to reach more readers than any other living dramatic critic, for, if he is at times too clever, he is, nevertheless, at all times entertaining. If he is at times irritating, he is, at the same time, provocative. If he occasionally deals flippantly in half-truths, it does not fol-

[19] *Ibid.*, pp. 222–23.

low that he is necessarily superficial. And if there are occasional gaps in his logic, there are few gaps in the soundness of his critical judgment. Journalistic, gay, intolerant, cruel, he is nevertheless highly intelligent, thoroughly informed, critically incorruptible, a serious and painstaking worker with a well-defined point of view, a true lover of the theatre.

CHAPTER TWO

The Nathan Critical Credo: The Art of Drama

WHAT you have read had been written when Burton Rascoe prophesied in *The American Mercury:*

> Some day a discerning aspirant for a Ph.D. will cull from the whole body of Nathan's work the aphorisms and observations which have nothing to do with the theatre or its art . . . And there will be left the great body of essays in dramatic criticism for which he has been famous, the earliest of which remain today more lively and more sensible than the celebrated dramatic essays of William Hazlitt or the equally celebrated dramatic essays of Jules Lemaître.[1]

Rascoe, writing these lines, was interested primarily in the matter culled; that is, the non-dramatic material.

---

[1] Roscoe, Burton, "Mencken, Nathan and Cabell," *The American Mercury*, XLIX (Mar., 1940), 367.

Our interest lies in what remains of the main body after the culling process. But Nathan's twenty-five books, deleted of everything not pertaining to the drama, purged of pleonasm, still would run to several thousand pages. Our task, then, is to condense further by grouping his criticism about its more important topics and giving the gist of his opinion on each of those topics—without sacrificing too much of his charm.

Perhaps this can't be done. Professor Goldberg, who attempted it on a small scale in 1926, and succeeded, warned that

> The dramatic criticism of George Jean Nathan is not a temple; it is a mosaic, made up of fragments of his personality, often tesselated carelessly, in many places cracked when examined too closely. Yet when viewed at the proper distance it assumes a design and a meaning.[2]

Strangely, Nathan wrote something very similar on the criticism of drama:

> Like tapestry, drama should not be scrutinized too closely. It should be pondered and criticized at several paces. It is not designed for near consideration; if analytically regarded at short range,

[2] Goldberg, *The Theatre of George Jean Nathan*, p. 4.

its woof and essential crudity dispel its creator's aim. That aim is solely to fashion a thing of suggestive illusion and beauty. The texture and the structure may in the eyes of too nosey criticism be ugly.[3]

And so, with a few misgivings, we proceed with our too nosey examination of the tesseræ of the Nathanian mosaic, trying meanwhile not to lose the concept of the whole.

DEFINITION OF GOOD DRAMA.—One indispensable tessera lends unity to all the rest. One sentence serves as the pitch-pipe which sets the pitch of the Nathanian symphony, and when all is finished this one tone echoes and re-echoes in our ears. Here is the single sentence to which Nathan has distilled his critical credo: *"Good drama is anything that interests an intelligently emotional group of persons assembled together in an illuminated hall."* [4] Here epitomized in the same sentence are his high-mindedness and his broad-mindedness, his tolerance which does not betray his emphasis on quality.

Not drama, we note, but "good drama." Not any group of persons but "an intelligently emotional group of per-

---

[3] *Materia Critica*, p. 242.
[4] *The Critic and the Drama*, p. 33. The italics are mine.

24

sons." Later, in discussing critical theories, he reiterates his stand. "Does the play interest, and whom? This seems to me to be the only doctrine of dramatic criticism that is capable of supporting itself soundly." And if the play interests, "does it interest inferior persons, or does it interest cultivated and artistically sensitive persons?" [5]

Good drama, then, must appeal to the aristocrat of taste and intellect or, better yet, to that delightful person who combines "the mind of a gentleman with the emotions of a bum," for Nathan frequently has declared that drama must be stimulating either (1) mentally or (2) physically; that "the business of the theatre and its drama is to quicken the mind or the memory, the heart or the pulse"; [6] that the drama which fails to do any or all of these things is not drama; that if it succeeds, we will know by "that precious after-image, . . . that day-after recollective warmth, which . . . is the stamp and mark of important drama." [7]

RULES OF DRAMATURGY.—"Good drama is *anything* which interests an intelligently emotional group of persons . . ."

Asked what constitutes a good play, Nathan wrote that there could be no such definition "save it be some

[5] *Ibid.,* p. 50.
[6] *The World in Falseface,* p. 32.
[7] *The Morning After the First Night,* p. 109.

such completely obvious and broadly empty one as is now and then dispensed by the writers of dramatic text books." [8] There always will be great dramatists who will break the shackles placed upon them by the theorists of drama:

> Thus, the definition chefs, full of Aristotle's unities, were put to rout by Georg Kaiser. Thus, full of wisdom about dramatic action, they were set to chasing their tails by Sierra and Shaw. And thus, full of dramaturgic rules and regulations, they have been flouted by Strindberg, Wedekind, Schnitzler, Evreinoff, Synge, Dunsany, Gorki, Pirandello, Hasenclever and many others. [9]

Here is a Nathan melody with which we soon become familiar. "Critical 'theories,' " he observed in perhaps his happiest variation of the theme, "with negligible exception seek to denude the arts of their splendid, gypsy gauds and to force them instead to don so many duplicated black and white striped uniforms." Yet drama has triumphed,

> and each triumph has been a derision of one of its most famous and distinguished critics. It

[8] *Art of the Night,* p. 17.
[9] *Ibid.,* p. 18.

triumphed, through Shakespeare, over Aristotle; it triumphed, through Lemercier, over Diderot; it triumphed, through Lessing, over Voltaire; it triumphed, through Hauptmann, over Sarcey and, through Schnitzler and Bernard Shaw, over Mr. Archer. The truth perhaps is that drama is an art as flexible as the imagination of its audiences. It is no more to be bound by rules and theories. Who so all-wise that he may say by what rules or set of rules living imaginations and imaginations yet unborn are to be fanned into theatrical flame? [10]

Even in the 1941–42 season, after he had devoted almost four decades to belittling the rules, Nathan found a majority of the critics contending that many of the plays by newer playwrights missed fire because their authors had not learned the business of sound construction. "This," replied Nathan in his best manner, "is sheer critical twaddle. The real trouble with the playwrights in question is not that they have not mastered the dramaturgical technique but that . . . their mental, spiritual, emotional and imaginative quotient is woefully deficient." [11]

Of course, he admits, a knowledge of technique helps.

[10] *The Critic and the Drama*, p. 48.
[11] "The Delusions of Musical Comedy," *The American Mercury*, LIII (Dec., 1941), 717.

But it is far from a prime essential. The genius may wave it aside. Gorki is a case in point. His best play is almost amateurish technically. Shaw is another. Most of his plays "would have been marked G-minus by professors of the George Pierce Baker school. . . ." And Wedekind's best play Nathan labels a technical botch. As for the misdirected indignation aimed at Saroyan, Nathan contends that if Saroyan wrote his plays according to the stricter dramaturgical formula, they would be unspeakably bad; their neglect of that formula he calls one of their chief virtues. "Some of the very worst plays in the theatre of the last few years have been technically perfect. And some of the very best have been as technically imperfect as Shakespeare's A *Midsummer Night's Dream*.[12]

A favorite device of his is to scoff at the devotees of the rule books by naming a generally accepted rule and a play which successfully ignores it. Any attempt to chart these from the various volumes must meet with incomplete results, for Nathan himself usually has been content to name a single play and allow the reader to carry forward the line of thought thus introduced. The following brief lists will be suggestive. In each instance the items listed were named by Nathan.

Requisite	Plays that refute the rule
Action	*Professor Bernhardi*

[12] *Ibid.*, p. 718.

Unity of time	*On Trial*
Love interest	*Pasteur*
A single dominating character	*Night Refuge*

Or, using the opposite approach, here are some taboos which have been successfully violated:

You can't	*They did*
Exceed three hours	*Strange Interlude*
Mix moods	*The Dream Play*
Contradict yourself	*Der Stein der Weisen*
Spring scenes without proper preparation	*Major Barbara* [13]
Obliterate most interesting figure in first act	*Little Eyolf*

The latest victim of Nathan's method of quoting exceptions to the so-called rules is Maxwell Anderson, who recently has told us that he "did discover that there were rules of playwriting which could not be broken." Nathan takes pleasure in appending noted exceptions to each of Anderson's eleven newly discovered rules. A single example will illustrate the continuing usefulness of the method:

[13] The scene between the thug and the Salvation Army girl in Act II. Nathan calls this "quite the most effective dramatic scene in the whole play."

ANDERSON. The protagonist of a play cannot be a perfect person. If he were he could not improve, *and he must come out at the end of the play a more admirable human being than he went in.*

NATHAN. Required playgoing for Mr. Anderson: *The Man Who Came to Dinner*, by Kaufman and Hart, to say nothing of Mr. Anderson's and Laurence Stallings' *What Price Glory?* [14]

Although praising Anderson for his integrity and high goal as a dramatist, Nathan finds him guilty of taking himself too seriously, of possessing a mind "critically incapable of meeting the demands it imposes upon itself." Fair warning to whoever discovers rules of playwriting which cannot be broken!

One might argue that this evidence is far from conclusive; but it is not Nathan's method to reveal to his readers the vast amount of scholarly data—or lack of it—which stands behind his conclusions. One might contend that some of these plays succeed despite their lapses, not because of them; to which Nathan probably would reply that more frequently the reverse is true, with rules reaping the praise for the success of plays in which the observance of dramaturgic rules was incidental. And when one

[14] "The People Versus the Playwrights," *The American Mercury*, LIV (Jan., 1942), 99.

has exhausted one's supply of arguments, he would reiterate along these lines:

> The theory that a wooden platform lit up by electricity and hung with strips of painted canvas and cheesecloth may respond only to a fixed and invariable set of rules is akin to the theory that a highly proficient actress with fat legs may be convincing in a romantic role. The truth of the matter being simply that a playwright may successfully do almost anything he chooses to do, provided only he has the necessary imagination and inventive skill for the doing.[15]

Our neat little case seems cut and dried. But Nathan suddenly explodes it with his advice to a hypothetical young critic:

> Don't go too far with the idea that there are no rules in the case of drama. There happen, fortunately or unfortunately, to be a few. Bumptiously to deny the existence of all such rules is to make one's self out a ninny. There are certain rules. What there are not, are commandments.[16]

[15] *Mr. George Jean Nathan Presents,* pp. 61–62.
[16] *Art of the Night,* p. 15.

So there are rules, after all. Nathan referred to them again in 1938, when he criticized Sinclair Lewis for his ignorance of "the fundamentals of dramatic composition," and in 1940, when he blasted Clifford Odets with these lines: "But the drama he seeks to serve waits patiently for him to grow up and to learn that only geniuses and imbeciles, in neither of which categories he finds himself, can flout all the rules and regulations." [17]

What are these rules? To Nathan the answer seems absurdly simple. "The basic laws, everyone knows; there is no need to write of them." And he doesn't. As for the by-laws, these are as fitful and as shifting as drama itself, forever changing. He points out the futility of fretting over rules which tomorrow "will be quite as empty and useless as an old tooth-powder can." So he treats these by-laws "with an air of dubiety and evanescence, and perhaps the flicker of a snicker." [18]

"TECHNIQUE WALLA-WALLA."—Dubiety also marks his approach to the subject of "blue-print dramaturgy." Concerning the work of the late Professor Baker who taught many a young Harvard and Yale man "the facile trick of building shows," he asked pointedly, "What

[17] *Encyclopaedia of the Theatre*, p. 291.
[18] *The House of Satan*, pp. 82–83.

is the use of teaching young men how to write plays if the young men have no plays to write?" [19]

One of Nathan's classic examples of the hollowness of mere technique is the English dramatist, Arthur Wing Pinero. Ten years before Pinero's death Nathan wrote of the dramatist's disintegration: [20]

> This disintegration is a peculiarly interesting thing: peculiarly interesting because it betrays how little, after all, mere great technical dexterity matters where the ever-changing years and times have brought with them no bounty of matured invention and fresh inspiration and marching novelty of thought.[21]

The difficulty of mastering dramatic technique is another matter that leaves him dubious. "If dramatic technique is, forsooth, the difficult thing some professors would have us believe, why is it that so many numskulls succeed at it?" [22] he asked, reasonably, submitting as numskull technicians Jean Webster, Catherine Chisholm Cushing, young Elmer Reizenstein, Augustus

[19] *Mr. George Jean Nathan Presents*, pp. 289–90.
[20] Goldberg remarked that these sentences "should be introduced into every course on drama and rememorized once every month."
[21] *Materia Critica*, p. 70.
[22] *Mr. George Jean Nathan Presents*, p. 244.

33

Thomas,[23] and others, and marshalling on the opposite side Shaw, Wedekind, Andreyev, Synge, Dunsany, and Tchekov, who "still have the pesky thing to master."

The following year he clarified his stand on Shaw's technique. "The truth about Shaw, of course, is that he understands the accepted structural technique so well that he is able to discard it." [24] Whether Andreyev, Synge, Dunsany, and Tchekov likewise have mastered and then discarded dramatic technique, he does not say. But in a later observation on Wedekind we see Nathan, finished carping at the purveyors of conventional artificiality—the form-minded critics and the overzealous formula playwrights—putting in a word for technique:

> Wedekind is the most cruel and forthrightly devastating dramatic mind that the stage of our immediate day has known. It is his misfortune that his technical equipment is not up to the demands of that mind. He is therefore doomed to pass into dramatic history as a mere symptom of what might have been an important talent.[25]

So Nathan tips his hat to dramatic technique, over-emphasized and without content an empty framework—

23 Thomas elsewhere was accorded the comment that his technique "is so perfect that it completely obscures his drama." (*Comedians All*, p. 143.)

24 *The Popular Theatre*, p. 25.

25 *The House of Satan*, p. 182.

the girders and the rafters—and yet, properly subordi-
nated, essential to supreme dramatic achievement.

DRAMATIC ACTION.—With the superb assurance
of youth, Nathan disposed of this topic in his first book:

> The question as to the indispensability of ac-
> tion in drama is ever with us. "Drama," says the
> iceman, "is not drama unless it has action." "Ac-
> tion," says the milkman, "is the chief requisite of
> drama." "Without action," says the policeman,
> "drama ceases to exist." And the simple truth is
> this: action is essential to plays in proportion to
> their intrinsic worthlessness.[26]

Having smashed this moot question of the centuries
with a single blow, he tossed it into a corner and dusted
off his hands. From time to time thereafter, however, he
found it necessary to rise to the defense of plays in which
the characters talked about the incidents without enact-
ing them. Patiently he pointed out to those still uncon-
vinced that this was the method of "eight out of ten of
the world's best plays," that only cheap melodrama visual-
izes every episode. "The drama of ideas is the drama of

[26] *Another Book on the Theatre*, p. 97.

35

the ear. The eye is the little brother of Kiralfy and Belasco." [27]

Then came Sierra's *Cradle Song*, its lethargy unbroken by any feeble stir of action, and Nathan was forced to recant. He did so promptly and with gusto:

> After many years of commentary in which such commonly spoken of "action" has been made the target of all sorts of ironic and facetious spontoons and djerrids, and in which the complete elimination of such absurd action has been rather obstreperously prayed for, it comes as something of a shock to find one suddenly getting one's wish and being bored half to death as a result. [28]

The year after he ruefully confessed to being bored half to death, he put in a word for the "good, old-fashioned, rousing climax" and the "Who-are-you? Hawkshaw-the-detective!" drama, and registered a complaint against the so-called refining tendency to foreshadow a dramatic climax and then to "shush it aside with a great show of tony disdain and substitute for it a nonchalant reference to the weather or a drawling allusion to the villain's spats." [29]

[27] *Mr. George Jean Nathan Presents*, p. 245.
[28] *The World in Falseface*, p. 167.
[29] *Materia Critica*, p. 190.

36

Several years later Pirandello's *Right You Are* provided another case in point, and Nathan, after spending two hours listening to "prolonged and unrelieved argumentation," was convinced that others beside Kiralfy and Belasco would do well to claim brotherhood with the drama of the eye. *Right You Are* is "mentally dramatic," Nathan admitted, but "after all," he protested, "the theatre calls for the use of the eye as well as the ear, and the Pirandello drama has the air of being written for intelligent blind men." [30]

But it was the French dramatists—or "undramatists"—of the last decade who drove him to what is probably his soundest expression on the subject. Referring to Shaw's widely quoted criticism of Sardou, that "his plan of playwriting was first to invent the action of his piece and then carefully to keep it off the stage and have it announced merely by letters and telegrams," Nathan added, "These grandchildren of Sardou have got rid of even the letters and telegrams." [31] Their abortive attempts at drama he regarded as empty parlor tricks unfair to the audience:

> If a play contains an important character and its
> subject matter calls for his presence, an audience
> has a right to see that character. . . If a play
> and its theme contain the germ of vital action, an

[30] *Art of the Night*, p. 150.
[31] *Testament of a Critic*, p. 142.

audience has a right to that action and it may not be airily philosophized into the wings with tea-table chatter. . . . The novel may simply tell the reader something; the stage must not only tell the spectator, it must also show him.[32]

In thus attacking bogus drama and defending the spectator's right to see characters and episodes called for by the subject matter, our erstwhile defender of the drama of the ear has not completely reversed his original opinion, for in his last expression on the subject to date he again defends the reasonable and skillful use of the absent character and the unseen incident, this time in Ibsen's *Little Eyolf,* Echegaray's *The Great Galeoto,* Hervieu's *The Enigma,* and in a number of Shaw's successful plays.

So it would seem that Nathan has come at last to the middle of the road; that here, as always, he shies from an inflexible rule, preferring as his criteria the logic and skill and charm—the art and the reasonableness—with which the device, whatever it may be, is employed.

DIALOGUE.—The "prolonged and unrelieved argumentation" of Pirandello has been succeeded these days by the garrulousness of Shaw's later plays and the ver-

[32] *Testament of a Critic,* p. 146.

bosity of Maxwell Anderson's poetic dramas. Nathan's observation that he finds their prolixity "something less than irresistible," eloquent though it may be, recalls his comment, years before, on understanding a drama spoken in a foreign language. He contended that a good play could be enjoyed even though one could not understand the language, for great drama is basically pantomime. "The greatest moments of any drama are those moments that constitute the spaces of silence between the speaking of one character and the speaking of another." [33]

Nathan's words on the spaces of silence are memorable. But there are other words of his which, quoted out of context, flatly contradict them. "Fine drama is born, first and last, of words, true words, vital and burning words, beautiful words. And there cannot be too many of them. . . . The great dramatist is, above everything else, an eloquent talker." [34]

Here he was defending J. B. Priestley's talkative *Dangerous Corner* by contending that words can express very definite, concrete action and by pointing out the "quivering dramatic and theatrical movement" of, for example, "the single wordy lament of the mother in *Riders to the Sea* or . . . Caesar's soliloquy before the Sphinx in Shaw's *Caesar and Cleopatra*. . ." The great dramatist

[33] *Materia Critica*, p. 33.
[34] *Passing Judgments*, p. 144.

is a great talker, he concluded, but the hack "is one who believes that human beings are only interesting and exciting when they aren't sitting quietly in a chair." [35]

CHARACTERIZATION.—"Sound character," Nathan wrote in an earlier book, "is the drama's most difficult achievement." [36] Consequently he takes issue time and again with the dramaturgic rule which oversimplifies the problem by calling for completely consistent characters, characters recognizable throughout the play by certain invariable reactions and characteristics: "a single idiosyncrasy in trousers." [37] To this school of dramaturgy he replies, "Clever playwrights may create characters who remain absolutely and entirely themselves from start to finish, but God is not quite so exact a craftsman." [38]

This tendency to create not characters but characteristics may be a carry-over from Victorian days. No carry-over from that much maligned era, however, are the dramas of "the vanished heroine," dramas of today whose leading women lack allure, whose leading men are merely leading men, not heroes. "What the drama cries for is a return to spiritual swords and purple, to softness, fineness, gentle wonder, and dignity," he admits in a softer

[35] *Passing Judgments*, p. 144.
[36] *The House of Satan*, p. 174.
[37] *Materia Critica*, p. 59.
[38] *Testament of a Critic*, p. 54.

moment. "What the drama needs are men and women of some romantic warmth and beauty and not these common, swearing, wisecracking, bawdy rats that today clutter up its stage." [39]

L'HOMME POUDRÉ AND HIS ART.—The powdered man, Nathan dubs the actor—the man whose profession demands that he paint his face; "that he pursue each day's work gazing more or less fondly at himself in a mirror for at least three-quarters of an hour"; that "night in and night out, . . . he must devote himself interestedly and even passionately to cuckooing . . . idiotic lines, sentiments and emotions"; the man, in short, who is steeped in artificiality year in and year out "until almost all that is real and natural in [him] becomes gradually metamorphosed into artificiality." [40] Greasepaint poison, he calls it, and contends that it corrupts nine out of ten actors, regardless of what they were before they took up the acting profession. Of course, there are "honorable exceptions," but greasepaint, to Nathan, continues to be synonymous with poison.

So much for the practitioners. What of the art which corrupts them? In the first place, Nathan (along with such great actors as Coquelin and Salvini, he is quick to

[39] *Ibid.*, p. 194.
[40] *Encyclopaedia of the Theatre*, pp. 157–60.

41

tell us) hoots at the notion that acting is an art. Among his reasons are these:

1. Acting lacks the universality of art. It is "more or less a thing sectional." [41]

2. It represents "the miscegenation of an art and a trade: of the drama and the theatre. Since acting must appeal to the many . . . it must, logically, be popular or perish. Surely no authentic art can rest or thrive upon such a premise." [42]

3. The best acting is a literal translation of the rôle the playwright has created. It requires the exercise of no creative imagination on the part of the actor.

4. The standards for criticizing acting are not standards which apply to the criticism of any authentic art. How is acting to be judged? Merely, says Nathan, in terms of "the particular critic's personal notion of how he, as a human being, would have cried, laughed and otherwise comported himself were he an actor and were he in the actor's rôle." [43]

5. The unionization of actors he terms the most ludicrous straw. "The artist not only does not care whether the hack starves to death; he hopes that he will starve to death, and the sooner the better." [44]

Nathan's most extensive denial that acting is an art

[41] *The Popular Theatre*, p. 156.
[42] *The Critic and the Drama*, p. 86.
[43] *Ibid.*, p. 96.
[44] *The House of Satan*, pp. 35–36.

appears in *The Critic and the Drama*, where it covers seventeen pages before concluding inconclusively: "If acting is an art—and I do not say that it might conceivably not be—. . ." [45]

Art or otherwise, acting receives further consideration from him. Few people, he admits, "know much about the matter and even what the few know is open to question." [46] The poorest possible judge of good acting is the actor himself, for acting, in Nathan's opinion, "is good acting in proportion to its effect upon the average audience. . ." [47] And his latest word on the subject echoes the sentiment: "Acting, whatever the academicians say, is . . . anything that gets over satisfactorily to an audience, even though professional actors, sitting in judgment, may moan mygod and work themselves into an indignant fit." [48]

He had a great deal more to say on the subject of acting—on the star system, which he damned vociferously for many years; on bad acting ruining good plays and, worse, good acting improving bad plays; on the importance of beauty in actresses and the unimportance of intelligence in actors. His comments on these subjects I feel justified in omitting as theatrical rather than dramatic criticism. By his own advice, "Acting should be seen,

[45] *The Critic and the Drama*, p. 103.
[46] *Encyclopaedia of the Theatre*, p. 7.
[47] *Mr. George Jean Nathan Presents*, p. 227.
[48] *Encyclopaedia of the Theatre*, p. 174.

not written about. Very often, indeed, God knows, it shouldn't even be seen." [49]

THE DEMOCRACY OF DRAMA.—In referring to the actor as "the child of the miscegenation of an art and a trade: of the drama and the theatre" and to acting as "a filter through which drama may be lucidly distilled for heterogeneous theatre-goers," [50] Nathan would seem to contend that the printed drama is aristocratic, the acted drama democratic.

But the distinction is not so simple. *All* great art, he points out, "is democratic in intention, if not in reward. . . . No great artist has ever in his heart deliberately fashioned his work for a remote and forgotten cellar. . . ." [51] In this respect the art of Shakespeare is no more democratic than the art of Wagner or Michelangelo, and though perhaps we enjoy Michelangelo in solitude, we enjoy Wagner as a group at least as frequently as we, as a group, enjoy Shakespeare.

There are other questions involved in this matter of group appeal—so many, in fact, that in 1918 he saw fit to devote an entire book to the subject. In *The Popular Theatre* he refers to the mob theatre—in this country or

[49] *Ibid.*, p. 11.
[50] *The Critic and the Drama*, p. 86.
[51] *Ibid.*, pp. 46–47.

any other—as "the barrack of balderdash, the cow-house of art," a theatre "whose constituents are interested solely in such dramatic pieces as reflect their own thoughts and emotions, as repeat to their ears those things they already know and feel," a theatre in which "the best in drama and dramatic literature must inevitably fail." And yet, in the same volume, Nathan denies that "the popular play is a bad play since it is written for the mob, and since the mob lowers automatically the intelligence of its component individuals."

> Take the lowest type of crowd imaginable, the type in which there is not more than one half-civilized man to every hundred, the crowd, for example, at a professional baseball game, and bundle that crowd bag and baggage into some great Carnegie Hall where they are playing Beethoven's Fifth. What would happen? At first, undoubtedly, a great deal of loud snickering . . . and let's get the hell out o' this morgue. And what then? A slowly settling mass . . . a crowd gradually shaming itself up to conduct of its more genteel and more cultured and more disciplined component parts—and a crowd listening at length if, true enough, not entirely with interest and sympathy, at least with open mind and in respectful silence.

Such a mob, instead of being lowered to its average indecorum and stupidity, as the professors maintain, is rather elevated in varying degree to its leaven of gentility and intelligence.[52]

More convincing is his simple statement four years later. "The fine drama or the fine piece of music does not make its auditor part of a crowd; it removes him, and every one else in the crowd, from the crowd, and makes him an individual. . . . The dramas of Mr. Owen Davis make crowds; the dramas of Shakespeare make individuals." [53]

What then? Is drama aristocratic? In the early pages of *The Popular Theatre* he pays tribute to the aristocracy of the theatre:

> . . . the theatre is to be necessarily regarded as an institution of an essential aristocracy: an aristocracy of beautiful letters, of ideas and wit, of viewpoint and philosophy. To hold the contrary, to hold the theatre a mere recess pasture for the potwallopers, a sauve dive for the proletarian taste on the loose, is to make shift to establish and appraise an art in terms of the number of its admirers. . . .
>
> From that side of the theatre which has been

[52] *The Popular Theatre*, pp. 33–34.
[53] *The Critic and the Drama*, pp. 39–40.

regarded as democratic, there has come down to us most of the rant and jabber, most of the pish and platitude. . . . From the side of aristocracy, from the theatre designed originally for the few, have come the Molières, . . . the Shakespeares, . . . the Ibsens, . . . the Hauptmanns, . . . and on down the list to the Bernard Shaws of the moment who, for their first hearings, have had to rely on private societies and closed doors.[54]

This, the reader feels, comes closest to fundamental Nathanism, for the man's inherent aristocracy is evident throughout his works. He does not write for the man in the street, he tells us, but for the man in the automobile. And though he praises democracy in the individual, he strongly mistrusts the mob. Even a beanbrain could sense the pride with which he wrote, in 1932, that the theatre had "become the theatre of the intelligent minority and only by so becoming may any theatre get within hailing distance of an art." [55]

Yet he has declared that no one completely the aristocrat can write real drama, for drama, says he, "is the stubborn, automatic echo in an artist's heart of the voice of the people from whom he has sprung." [56]

[54] *The Popular Theatre,* pp. 18–19.
[55] *The Intimate Notebooks of George Jean Nathan,* p. 183.
[56] *The Theatre, the Drama, the Girls,* p. 180.

47

Obviously, then, we can eliminate wholly neither democracy nor aristocracy from our concept of drama—from Nathan's concept of drama. We must recognize, with him, the conflicting presence of both:

> Drama is, in essence, a democratic art in constant brave conflict with aristocracy of intelligence, soul and emotion. When drama triumphs, a masterpiece like *Hamlet* comes to life. When the conflict ends in a draw, a drama half-way between greatness and littleness is the result—a drama, say, such as *El Gran Galeoto*. When the struggle ends in defeat, the result is a *Way Down East* or a *Lightnin'*. This, obviously, is not to say that great drama may not be popular drama, nor popular drama great drama. . . Drama that has come to be at once great and popular has ever first been given the imprimatur, not of democratic souls, but of aristocratic. . . . In our own day, the drama of Hauptmann, Shaw and the American O'Neill has come into its popular own only after it first achieved the imprimatur of what we may term the unpopular, or undemocratic, theatre. Aristocracy cleared the democratic path for Ibsen, as it cleared it, in so far as possible, for Rostand and Hugo von Hofmannsthal.[57]

[57] *The Critic and the Drama*, pp. 29–30.

LIBRARY DRAMA.—Into any consideration of the democracy of drama, with its necessary deviations into crowd psychology, will creep the question of library drama. In weighing the relative merits of such drama and the acted play, we are not concerned with those "dramatic hybrids" in which the materials of a novel or a biography have been forced into a form which is dramatic only in the arrangement of the lines on the printed page. We are concerned, instead, with theatrically sound plays. Nathan assures us that good drama is also good literature. The question, then, is whether good drama should be read in the library or be seen on the stage.

Here is another problem with which he tangled time and again two decades ago, not always arriving at the same conclusion, and a subject—like the aristocracy of drama—to which he has devoted little space since 1922. Perhaps he considers the matter settled. Or perhaps beyond solution.

His definition of good drama as anything that interests an intelligently emotional group of persons assembled together in an illuminated hall practically precludes the "comfortable chair under a reading lamp" which three years earlier he had called "the only place for worthwhile drama." [58] *The Popular Theatre* is a con-

[58] *Comedians All*, p. 167.

tinual outcry against the limitations which the theatre places on the imagination of the theatregoers—against "the windblown hair of Hope Langham, . . . held at the appropriate windblown length by a more or less visible black thread"—against the "field of baldheads" which the "dreaming vision" must cross to reach the stage—the stage with its Mediterranean sky "that nine times in ten is rich in grease-spots and fly-specks." In short, he concluded, "Fine dramatic literature . . . belongs not upon the stage, but in the library. . . . Some plays are too beautiful for the spoken stage; they are orchestrated alone for the strings of the silent imagination." [59]

Four years later he was equally eloquent in his defense of the acted play. In a chapter of *The Critic and the Drama* entitled "The Place of the Theatre," he lauds the contribution of the theatre to the play, pointing out that a drama *read* is enriched by a single imagination, that of the reader, whereas a drama *produced* is enriched by the imaginations of at least five persons—the actor, the scene designer, the musician, the costumer, and the producing director—all five of whom first read the play and then combined their ideas, selecting only the best.

The theatre brings to the art of drama concrete movement, concrete color, and concrete final ef-

fectiveness: this, in all save a few minor particu-
lars. The art of drama suffers, true enough, when
the theatre, even at its finest, is challenged by it
to produce the values intrinsic in its ghost of a
dead king, or in its battle on Bosworth Field, or in
its ship torn by the tempest, or in its fairy wood
on midsummer night, or in its approaching tread
of doom of the gods of the mountain. But for
each such defeat it prospers doubly in the gifts
that the theatre brings to it. . . . To say that the
reading imagination of the average cultured man
is superior in power of suggestion and depiction
to the imagination of the theatre is idiotically to
say that the reading imagination of every average
cultured man is superior in these powers to the
combined theatrical imaginations of Gordon
Craig, Max Reinhardt and Eleanora Duse operat-
ing jointly upon the same play.[60]

So Nathan wrote in 1922. Since then he has not written
extensively on the subject. But this observation may be
misleading. True, he has not theorized on the problem
at great length, but he has dealt with it even more directly
in criticizing acting, direction, and production. He has
dealt with it, too, in maintaining that the merits of a play
are to be determined on the basis of the play itself, not

[60] *The Critic and the Drama*, pp. 69–70.

on its interpretation or misinterpretation by any given troupe of actors.

Professor Goldberg has summarized the situation most aptly in his comment that Nathan's "whole corpus of criticism is a remarkable devastation of the stage as betrayer of the drama." [61]

FLEXIBLE MOUNTAINS.—A brief digression into theatrical criticism is necessary to remove the inference of meticulosity from Nathan's comment on the fly-specked Mediterranean sky. Contrary to the foregoing impression, he is a conscientious objector to the too-perfect theatre. He feels that recent improvements in scenery and electrical equipment have made the illusion too complete, have taken from the theatre "its fine old youthful barbarism, . . . all the old flaws that made it dear to the heart—. . . and its erstwhile wonderful old smell." [62] His plea is not for too-realistic scenery and a fly-speckless sky. His plea for the theatre runs like this: "Let us have back its old canvas mountains that bend in the middle when the villain leans against them. . . *They* are the soul of the theatre!" [63]

[61] Goldberg, *The Theatre of George Jean Nathan*, p. 109.
[62] *The Theatre, the Drama, the Girls*, pp. 167–68.
[63] *Ibid.*, pp. 175–76.

ART OF THE NIGHT.—It was not a whim that caused
Nathan to name one of his books *Art of the Night*. It was
not a whim that caused him to tack onto his definition of
drama the phrase "in an illuminated hall." Drama, in his
opinion, cannot stand the light of day. "One thin shaft of
daylight streaming suddenly into a theatre would kill the
greatest dramatic scene that a Hauptmann ever wrote." [64]
And again: "The acted drama prospers in proportion to
the artificiality and unreality of its immediate surroundings." [65]

It is not difficult, then, to imagine his stand on outdoor drama. The fact that Euripides originally was played
out-of-doors Nathan considers a very poor excuse for playing Euripides—or anyone else—out-of-doors today. "I
am disposed to regard outdoor drama as of a kidney with
indoor baseball." [66]

ON FEMALE PLAYWRIGHTS.—Like other bachelors
whose extensive knowledge of women often surpasses the
benedicks' intensive knowledge in the same field, Nathan
enjoys assuming a pose of ignorance where anything fe-

[64] *The World in Falseface*, p. 24.
[65] *Another Book on the Theatre*, p. 18.
[66] *Ibid.*, p. 16.

53

male is concerned. Why are playwrights in petticoats inferior to playwrights in pants? Nathan doesn't know. And he assuredly isn't going to write a scholarly treatise implying that he does. But he manages, between frequent I-may-have-been-mistakens, to venture some shrewd guesses.

Guess No. 1. Taken as a group, plays by women do not measure up to plays by men because "a woman dramatist seldom succeeds in mastering an economy of the emotions." When a woman sits down to write a play, she picks up a given emotion and stretches it, mauls it, drags it around by the hair until her drama verges on melodrama and her comedy on farce. Nathan carefully differentiates between Strindberg's intentional over-intensification of emotion, which he calls a deliberate dramaturgical technique, and the melodramatic excesses of—say—Lillian Hellman in *The Children's Hour*, *The Little Foxes*, and *Watch on the Rhine*. With a woman playwright, he contends, overemotionalism is unintentional or unavoidable. It is the feminine blind spot.

Guess No. 2. Women playwrights fail to see their leading characters objectively. This is not true of women novelists, and why it should be true of women playwrights baffles the bachelor critic.

Guess No. 3. Riding a prejudice is the final fault. It "appears to be almost impossible for a serious American woman playwright to handle a theme save she be positively committed that one side of it is absolutely right and the other side absolutely wrong. There can be no middle ground, no flicker of doubt, no dispute of reason or justice. Black must be black, white must be white. And however artfully she may try to conceal her arbitrariness, her womanish prejudice remains transparent." [67]

After which the gentleman critic bows in apology to Miss Hellman, whom he considers "not only far to the forefront of her local playwriting sex but very considerably in the van of a sufficient number of the lesser uglier gender."

INTELLECTUAL DRAMA.— Another canon in the Nathan credo concerns the absence of ideas in drama. Drama, he believes, contains few ideas; nor should it contain any. A person entering a theatre should check his mind at the door, just as he checks his mind before going onto a dance floor. "The theatre is, above everything else, a pleasure temple: the mind has no place in it." [68] Thus he takes issue with his fellow critics who constantly are clamoring for intellectual drama.

Not only is drama wholly adequate and pleasing without intelligence, drama—and all fine art—insults the intelligence. "It deliberately spits in the eye of intelli-

[67] *The Entertainment of a Nation*, p. 36.
[68] *The Theatre, the Drama, the Girls*, p. 273.

55

gence. The imperishable tragedies of Shakespeare ask us to believe in ghosts and witches, . . . and Wagner asks us to believe, in *Lohengrin*, that a dove can pull a boat." [69] If any play lives on in the theatre solely because of its thought, he adds, its name escapes him.

He analyzes the intellectual content of six of the world's finest plays and reports his findings:

> 1. *Electra.* Intellectual content: If a woman murders her husband, both her son and daughter will grow to hate her and the son may end up by vengefully killing her. Emotional content: 100 per cent.
>
> 2. *Oedipus.* Intellectual content: Incest is likely to have tragic consequences. Emotional content: 100 per cent.
>
> 3. *Medea.* Intellectual content: Hell knoweth no fury like a mother the lives of whose children are threatened. Emotional content: 100 per cent.
>
> 4. *Hamlet.* Intellectual content: A young man's natural impulse is to avenge his father's murder. To be successful in the enterprise, he must be pretty subtle and damned canny. Emotional content: 95 per cent, even not overlooking the wisdom implicit in certain dialogue passages.
>
> 5. *King Lear.* Intellectual content: A man

[69] *The House of Satan*, pp. 15–16.

overburdened with troubles may lose his equi-
librium and even his reason. Emotional content:
100 per cent.

    6. *Romeo and Juliet.* Intellectual content:
Love, however star-crossed, conquers all, even in
death. Emotional content: 100 per cent. Maybe
even 102 per cent.[70]

What was true of ancient Greece and Elizabethan England holds today. Nathan goes on to analyze the twenty
plays that have achieved the longest runs in the modern
American theatre and finds their intellectual content
negligible, equally as negligible as the intellectual content of some of the better successful new plays—*Claudia,
The Corn Is Green, Old Acquaintance, My Sister Eileen,
The Eve of St. Mark.*

    By its nature, drama is not and never can be a vehicle
for the expression of substantial and profound ideas.
Even a Shakespeare could not keep an audience awake
were he to attempt seriously to treat in dramatic form
"the influence of the conception of evolution on philosophy." Far better material for the stage are "such easy
speculations and second-hand quasi-philosophies as
Andreyev's on the burden of religion, as Dunsany's on
fate, as Brieux's on heredity, and Galsworthy's on social

[70] "Emotion Rules the Stage," *The American Mercury,* LII (May, 1941),
617.

economics." [71] And better yet are emotion and humor.

Such is Nathan's message to playwrights who would write "important" drama and to critics who would praise their efforts. Together they are doing serious injury to American drama. Or, as he puts it, "A present trouble with the American drama is that too many of its authors are trying to write ideas instead of plays." [72]

That the theatre is the "bourse of platitudes" is, he admits, itself platitudinous. "In the entire history of the theatre there has never been produced a play, great or puny, that . . . presents a single new contribution to human thought." [73] By the time any philosophic idea reaches the point of production on the stage, that idea is "already a great-grandfather." Consequently those playwrights who insist on dealing with ideas—necessarily platitudinous by the nature of the theatre—find that their plays, as Nathan puts it, ". . . take on the aspect of so many rush telegrams, delivered by a breathless messenger-boy, which contain information that the recipient has read in day before yesterday's newspaper, and not been the least interested in." [74]

Although the stage is not the place for ideas or for intelligence, it is the place "for a deft and sagaciously de-

[71] *Comedians All*, p. 117.
[72] *The Intimate Notebooks of George Jean Nathan*, p. 153.
[73] *Art of the Night*, p. 193.
[74] *The House of Satan*, p. 21.

ceptive simulacrum of intelligence." [75] This simulacrum of intelligence consists in fooling the public in the matter of platitudes. The dramatist "is, in a way of speaking, a prestidigitator of platitudes: one whose infinite legerdemain of metaphor, fancy, wit and surface originality is successful constantly in making the ever-present platitudes seem to disappear." [76]

Thus a dramatist may exercise his intelligence.

"DRAMA IS EMOTION."—If there is little or no place in drama for intelligence, there is ample place for what Nathan refers to as emotional intelligence. When a man enters the theatre, he voluntarily surrenders his mind to his emotions. But his emotions are not the naïve and unrestricted emotions of the Harlem shoe-dealer or the flapper. The ideal theatregoer—if we may refer once more to his definition of drama— is "intelligently emotional." This, Professor Goldberg points out, "is, for his [Nathan's] peculiar personality, the wise course between academic solemnity on the one hand and, on the other, adolescent gush." [77]

So much for the emotional response of the theatre

[75] *Materia Critica*, p. 11.
[76] *Ibid.*, p. 70.
[77] Goldberg, *op. cit.*, p. 26.

audience. The precedence which emotions take over intelligence in characterization is aptly demonstrated in Nathan's comment on Macbeth:

> No matter how poorly the characters of drama reason, the demands of drama are fully satisfied so long as their emotions are, or at least seem to be, reasonable. . . . Macbeth is a simpleton, but his emotions are those of a great man, hence he is a great dramatic character. And it is the same with most of the great characters of drama. It is almost impossible to imagine a fine play built around, say, Kant or Hegel as a philosopher. The theatre has no call for such heroes. Its heroes must think with their hearts and feel with their minds.[78]

To feel with their minds. That is the function of the dramatist, the actor, and the theatregoer, for the "first and encompassing aim" of drama is "a direct appeal to the emotions." [79]

It is this appeal to the emotions that brings immortality. The dramas of classic Greece, the dramas of Ibsen and Hauptmann, and dramas like *Cyrano de Bergerac* and *Riders to the Sea*, with their profound emotions,

[78] *The House of Satan*, p. 17.
[79] *The Critic and the Drama*, p. 35.

have more life in them than the dialectic dramas and, Nathan predicts, "will doubtless sing their songs to future stages long after a hundred *Getting Marrieds, Apple Carts, Strifes* and *Justices* have disappeared from the face of the theatre," for it is the absence of profound emotion that "so quickly stales much of the drama of men like Shaw [80] and Galsworthy." [81]

THE THEME, THE MESSAGE, AND THE SUBJECT.—Another plank in Nathan's platform allows the playwright absolute liberty in his choice of theme. This does not mean, of course, that Nathan approves of the tendency of American dramatists to stretch a theme by generalizing, in the mistaken belief that the theme, having achieved a wider application, thereby increases in importance. Nor does he approve of playwrights who feel it their duty to "say something" when they have nothing to say—S. N. Behrman, by way of recent example—who, as Nathan phrases it, "has strainfully lugged in his big Say like a piano-mover and dumped it into his comedies with such a bang that it has frightened the wits, to say nothing of the happy and graceful tranquillity, out of them." [82]

Here he is not discrediting plays which do say some-

[80] The more emotional *Candida* is a noteworthy exception to this generalization on Shavian drama, Nathan added.
[81] *The Intimate Notebooks of George Jean Nathan*, p. 271.
[82] *Encyclopaedia of the Theatre*, p. 320.

thing. Whether or not he would agree with the late William Archer, who held that one of the three requisites of a great play is a definite message from the playwright to his audience, Nathan states that obviously he prefers plays that "really say something"to those that do not. But this dragged in "importance," this afterthought theme, is another matter.

Most of these playwrights who have nothing to say, he adds, "believe it absolutely necessary that, whatever the rest of their plays may be like, they must irrespectively say it about Capitalism, Communism, or My God What Is Going To Become of Civilization." [83] And so we have plays of "social significance." Elsewhere he lists two other complaints against playwrights, critics and theatregoers who serve social significance. First, they consign to the junk-heap any play which lacks social significance, thereby disposing of many of the world's best plays. Secondly, they defend any play glorifying the man in overalls and condemn as "Ivory Tower bunk" and "commercial claptrap" any play depicting the boss trying to reason with his men for the good of the company.

Nathan sounds an extra hoot for those critics who naïvely believe that a big theme begets an important play and in their ignorance give the nod to poor plays like *Flight to the West* or *Marching Song*, whose themes carry journalistic weight, over the well-wrought *Claudia*,

[83] *Ibid.*, p. 318.

with its simple theme of a young girl's adaptation to marriage. He abhors the "general modern tendency to evaluate drama in proportion to the size of the theme rather than in proportion to the merit with which a theme, big or little, has been treated." And he finds it necessary to remind his critical brethren that "some of the world's finest plays have had themes relatively insignificant in comparison with some of the world's worst plays . . ." [84]

Continuing with this matter of saying something—continuing, more specifically, with Archer's requirement of a definite message—we find Nathan in 1927 terming the theory of the message of art ridiculous:

> As ridiculous as the theory that great art exercises an ennobling influence [85] upon man and inculcates in him a prompt and overwhelming passion for close psychic association with God, the angels and the League for the Enforcement of Prohibition, is the sister theory that great art must inevitably carry a message to man. Great art, in point of fact, carries no such thing; rather is it great art for the directly opposite reason. . . . Art, precisely speaking, has no other actual mes-

[84] *The Entertainment of a Nation*, pp. 38-39.
[85] A great part of Nathan's *The House of Satan* is, as the title suggests, an attempt to debunk the so-called ennobling influence of the theatre.

sage than its internal dignity and splendor. What, conceivably, is the nature of the "message" of *Huckleberry Finn*, of the *Iliad*, of Michelangelo's sculpture, of a Brahms trio, of Raphael's portrait of himself, or of the Grand Central Station? The message in each of these cases is simply, and nothing more than, this: that a great artist has achieved perfect form in his own particular domain of art. That is the only message that real art carries. The messages that certain critics speak of—these critics who conceive of art as a branch of the Western Union—are reserved for imitations of authentic art. Maeterlinck's *Blue Bird*, Gounod's *Nazareth* and Longfellow's *Hiawatha* have messages and duly convey them to the boobs, but Shakespeare's *Twelfth Night*, a Beethoven fantasia and Chaucer's *The Assembly of Fowls* have no more of a message than so many brilliant stars in the heavens.[86]

There, in less than three pages, is Nathan's answer to William Archer's "Western Union" philosophy of art.

So much for the message of the play. The subject— or rather, the unimportance of the choice of subject— he stresses in his second latest book. Here he calls to task Brooks Atkinson of the New York *Times*, who

[86] *Land of the Pilgrims' Pride*, pp. 95–97.

64

wrote of *Abe Lincoln in Illinois:* "In judging a work of art, the choice of subject is the first fact of importance. Everything else derives from that." Nathan takes issue with Mr. Atkinson:

> What kind of aesthetic rumble-bumble is that, my dear fellow? In judging a work of art, the choice of subject is a fact of relatively minor importance. The subject of one of Rembrandt's finest works of art is an old woman cleaning her fingernails. The subject of one of Bach's is a protest against the drinking of coffee. . . . If Sherwood's play is fine stuff because in Lincoln he has chosen "one of the most glorious subjects to be found in the common domain of playwriting," then surely most of the feeble plays that have been written about one of the even more glorious subjects to be found in the common domain of playwriting—Jesus Christ, to wit—are even finer stuff.[87]

Summarizing these scattered remarks on the theme, the message, and the subject, we find that Nathan allows the playwright free choice of theme but disapproves of generalizing a theme to stretch its application and disapproves, too, of playwrights who feel duty bound to say

[87] *Encyclopaedia of the Theatre,* p. 445.

something when they have nothing to say. He believes, further, that great art need carry no message and that the choice of subject is unimportant, its treatment being the thing that matters.

PROPAGANDA PLAYS.—Probably least of any living critic would George Jean Nathan be taken in by propaganda. He is the man, then, to rise to its defense; and this he does in *The Autobiography of an Attitude*:

> I cannot entirely agree with those critics who inveigh against propaganda in art and who maintain that propaganda, having no place in art, ruins art in its presence. Great art, they contend, proves nothing, should seek to prove nothing, may prove nothing. Many of the world's masterpieces confound such critics. *Hamlet* proves that it is futile for men to fight destiny as *Macbeth* proves that evil thought and wrongdoing can profit no man. *The Mikado* is veiled propaganda against certain British weaknesses and peccadillos, as are also *Iolanthe, Pinafore* and *The Pirates of Penzance*. . . . There is social and political propaganda in Swift's *Gulliver's Travels*, as there are political plea and argument in Shaw's finest play, *Caesar and Cleopatra*. . . .[88]

[88] *The Autobiography of an Attitude*, pp. 158–59.

At the risk of being labeled a quibbler, I should like to inquire whether proving "that it is futile for men to fight destiny" and "that evil thought and wrongdoing can profit no man" constitute a theme, a message, or propaganda. Nathan's comments here lend themselves to double interpretation, and to consider the themes of *Hamlet* and *Macbeth* as propaganda is to place a slightly unusual connotation on the word. However, since this question does not arise elsewhere in his works, there is no need to indulge in excessive literalness at this point. On the whole, his meaning is obvious: great art can and does propagandize.

But to what avail does drama propagandize? After examining the entire range of modern world drama—modern in the broader sense—he finds only five plays which have "even faintly exercised any influence upon persons other than playwrights and critics or upon institutions other than the theatre itself . . ." [89] They are Beaumarchais' *The Marriage of Figaro*—1784, Hugo's *Hernani*—1830, Ibsen's *A Doll's House*—1879, Brieux's *Damaged Goods*—1902, and Bernstein's *Après Moi*—1911. Of these, the influence of *A Doll's House* and *Après Moi* is possibly doubtful, and the influence of *Damaged Goods* was momentary. As for the quality of these dramas, the first three we recognize as superior, but the two plays of the present century Nathan labels trashy.

[89] *Encyclopaedia of the Theatre*, p. 226.

Probably the outstanding propaganda play of the last decade —from the point of view of its long run, which of course has nothing to do with its quality—is *Tobacco Road*. But the pitiable people it portrays have not profited in the least. "It seems to be the fate of the drama," Nathan concludes, referring to drama as a whole, "that audiences will frequently accept and abide by its artistic and cultural injunctions but seldom, if ever, by its political, social, religious, or economic." [90]

Drama, then, can and does propagandize—but to little or no avail. Not that he bewails the situation. Fourteen years earlier he rejoiced in the decreased popularity of propaganda plays as "an encouraging sign of improvement in the quality of the American theatrical audience." [91] One can imagine his disgust when, in the New York World's Fair year of 1939, many professional reviewers hailed *The American Way* ("two hundred thousand dollars' worth of chronological flag-waving"), as a great American patriotic document. He lost no time in pointing out with cosmopolitan detachment that these same critics "are loudest in their sardonic derogation of the open-and-shut propaganda drama in Germany and Russia." [92]

The American Way, alas, was only a preview. And Na-

[90] *Ibid.*, p. 227.
[91] *The House of Satan*, p. 286.
[92] *Encyclopaedia of the Theatre*, pp. 136–38.

than, who in 1925 had defended propaganda, and who by 1940 was seriously questioning its value, found himself in 1942 frantically sticking his finger in the dyke, endeavoring to hold back the flood of propaganda plays that threatens to sweep before it many of the advances which the American theatre has made in the last twenty years. Thus the ever-changing theatre causes the critic to appear to contradict himself.

Always the showman, this time Nathan chooses to get his point across by telling us a story—a delightful little story of a summer evening, of excellent champagne, of many lovely young girls, and the orchestra softly playing a Strauss waltz. He walked over and sat with Dorothy Thompson. "What," she instantly demanded, "is your opinion of Molotov, Voroshilov, Kalinin, Malenkov and Timoshenko?"

"I read Sean O'Casey's new play, *Purple Dust*, this afternoon," he answered. "It is rich in poetic imagination."

Miss Thompson looked at him over her champagne glass with profound disgust. "What is a mere play, even one by O'Casey, in times like these!"

Nathan told her that his job is dramatic criticism, and the play interested him.

"A critic!" she scoffed. "There is no place today for a mere kibitzer in life."

What Nathan refrained from saying—until publication—was that "the only perceptible difference between us was that Dorothy was a critic-kibitzer in the field of war and politics whereas I was one in the field of the theatre and drama." Instead, he tells us, he bowed elegantly at the middle, kissed her on each cheek, and departed for the bar, where he and the bartender pondered the fate of the artist, shunned when he alone could give this famished world "even a little glimpse of the old peace and fineness and beauty." Nathan went on to deplore the general impatience these days with any novelist or playwright who does not select his theme from the daily newspaper. "A dubious journalism has usurped the chair of Melpomene; . . . Calliope grows to look more and more like Winston Churchill; . . . Terpsichore runs a Bundles for Britain ball; Erato chalks derisory limericks about Hitler on the lavatory wall . . . The Dorothy Thompsons and their boy-friends may write their heads off and yet they can no more bring down a single Messerschmitt with their propaganda screeches than they can bring up the estate of the drama with their propaganda plays like *Another Sun*." [93]

To most of this many critics, Richard Lockridge among them, take exception. Mr. Lockridge argues that any playwright whose characters are contemporary men must take into consideration what those men are thinking and talking about, and there can be little doubt that war is the thought uppermost in the minds of men today. "You may,

[93] *The Entertainment of a Nation*, p. 29.

as O'Neill presumably is doing, write about men who lived in the sixteenth century or may live in the twenty-second. But you can not write about men sitting in drawing rooms in 1942 and talking about things which concern men in 1942, without writing about things which are also in today's newspapers." Furthermore, Lockridge adds in a telling sentence, "An event is not necessarily trivial merely because it is today's event, and a play written about it need not be." [94]

But Nathan delves into his storehouse of dramatic data and pulls out two important facts. First, he reminds us, it was the ivory tower which gave the theatre its superior plays in the last war. And it is the ivory tower which, thus far, has produced the superior plays of World War II. Here is a fact not yet recognized by "the otherwise meritorious Sherwoods, Behrmans and the like" who, in the belief that during this crisis only plays with political, racial, or chauvinistic messages are desirable, are busily turning out plays "that are little more than soapboxes full of grease-paint." Nathan weighs their propagandizing efforts against the ivory tower variety and finds that propaganda weighs light.

Sherwood's topical *There Shall Be No Night* is surely no strict critical match for either Saroyan's

[94] Lockridge, Richard, "The Nathan Phenomenon," *The Saturday Review of Literature*, XXV (Jan. 24, 1942), 12.

The Time Of Your Life or *The Beautiful People*, neither of which concerns itself with the immediate world's alarms. Behrman's *The Talley Method*, with its Nazi metaphors, surely does not compare in dramatic quality even with *Claudia*, which is a simple play about a young girl's adaptation to marriage. Rice's *Flight To The West*, bursting with anti-Nazi sentiments, is critically as inferior to his own pacific *Street Scene*, even to his own more pacific *The Left Bank*, as Anderson's *Candle In The Wind*, similarly bursting with anti-Nazi indignations, is to Anderson's own more tranquil *Saturday's Children*, *Elizabeth the Queen*, or *Mary of Scotland*. And Lillian Hellman's *Watch On The Rhine* can't compare in any really sound critical estimate with either Lillian Hellman's *The Little Foxes* or *The Children's Hour*.[95]

There have been good propaganda plays, he assures us, *but*—and this is his second point—they have been written considerably *after* the event. "Meditation and reflection have thus distilled what was mere stark propaganda into the tincture of philosophical dramatic literature. Heat makes reporters; calm makes poets." [96]

[95] "The People Versus The Playwrights," *The American Mercury*, LIV (Jan., 1942), 103.
[96] *The Entertainment of a Nation*, p. 31.

Heat makes propaganda plays, and the Nathan temperament is one of cool detachment. "The great problems of the world—social, political, economic and theological—do not concern me in the slightest. . . . What concerns me alone is myself, and the interests of a few close friends. For all I care, the rest of the world may go to hell at to-day's sunset." [97] He dashed off these lines in deliberate insolence twenty years ago, but they offer a key today to his comments on propaganda. The man and his criticism are cold—like a diamond—brilliantly, intensely cold.

To summarize, Nathan has not arbitrarily ruled propaganda out of every artistic endeavor. He admits that there are good propaganda plays, but they are plays written after an interval of time has allowed warm feelings to grow cool and judgment to mature. Furthermore, as propaganda they have accomplished nothing. And finally, this insidious rapid growth of propaganda weeds could choke out the flowering of the American theatre. In Nathan's theatre first things come first. A play first of all must be a good play, one capable of holding the interest of an intelligent audience. If it is, propaganda will not harm it; if it is not, propaganda will not save it.

WAR PLAYS.—During World War I, Nathan wrote that nothing is so immediately inimical to the powers of

[97] *The World in Falseface*, pp. x–xii.

imagination as colossal grandeur or stupendous tragedy. "No man ever imagined a great poem while his eyes swept the vast magnificence of a Grand Canyon . . . Thus, a great and dazzling canvas of war—such a war as that now raging in the world—blinds imagination rather than stimulates it . . . Years must elapse, and perspective intervene, before it may give birth to a great novel, a great poem, a great drama." *Riders to the Sea* grew out of the grief of one peace-time mother. But "a hundred thousand wartime mothers' grief gives theme-being to nothing save tin-pot melodrama like *Seven Days' Leave* or *The White Feather*." [98]

Twenty-four years later he could use the same phrase to describe like results. "They have turned the once proud theme of war—a theme that contributed to Greece's dramatic glory—into the leit-motif of tin-pot melodrama . . ." [99] Added now to the evil pressure of moral indignation and to the rhapsodic treatises on noble self-sacrifice is a new danger—enemy bombing. One well placed bomb can accomplish in two seconds what the heroine and the playwright could not achieve in two hours: complete metamorphosis of the scalawag into the fair-haired boy. Nathan's comment on this bit of machination is real dramatic criticism: "The measure of a good

[98] *The Popular Theatre*, p. 201.
[99] "Drama As a War Atrocity," *The American Mercury*, LIII (Nov., 1941), 618.

dramatist is to be found in the manner and means by which he delineates flux in character. The good dramatist maneuvers it internally; the bad dramatist, externally. The mental and psychic changes of the heroes of fine drama are not wrought by bombs . . . or revolvers pressed against the midriff or rescues from the East River . . . They occur in the great inner silences, with the quiet and stealthy tread of either tame or wild tigers." [100]

As an aside on the bomb question, he deplores playwrights who confuse noise with drama and consequently deafen their audiences with the racket of off-stage Stukas, Heinkels, and Messerschmitts. Except for the single brief uproar in *What Price Glory?*, he cannot recall a single excellent war play of all history that was not practically soundless.

Such trifles aside, the big question remains: is war a fit subject for the theatre? His answer is emphatic and positive.

It is commonly asserted that war is too big a subject for the drama, that the theatre and its few allotted hours are too constricted for so great a subject, and that as a consequence the stage and drama have had to fall back on its lesser aspects. This, of course, is the sheerest nonsense. The point is, rather, that war is too big a subject only for too

[100] *Ibid.*, p. 620.

little dramatists and that it is they who perforce have had to fall back on its minor incidentals. War was not too big a subject for the Greek dramatists, nor for Shakespeare, Schiller, or the Shaw of *Saint Joan*. It is simply too big for the Sherriffs, Howards, Brennans and the like.[101]

For that dramatist large enough to handle the subject, Nathan has a suggestion as to treatment.

> There may be food for some meditation in the circumstance that the only two American plays of any real or relative critical quality that resulted from World War I were cast very largely in the comic mold, to wit, the before-noted exceptional *What Price Glory?* of Anderson and Stallings and the lesser *Johnny Johnson* of Paul Green. There may be even more food for meditation in the circumstance that the only Central European play of any critical quality that resulted from that same war was also cast in the comic mold, to wit, *The Good Soldier Schweik* of Carl Zuckmayer. And there may be quite as much food for meditation in the circumstance that the dismal gravity of the French contrived to produce only second- and

[101] *Ibid.*, p. 621.

third-rate plays at best and that, with all of England's gravity, the only reputable play to come out of that nation in turn was the witty *Heartbreak House* of Bernard Shaw.[102]

SINCERITY.—From the beginning, Nathan has questioned the desirability of sincerity in writers. His first book devoted to the subject a chapter entitled *The Unimportance of Being Earnest,* in which he ventured the opinion that seven-tenths of the world's literature was written by insincere scalawags.

"Your true artist is seldom, if ever, sincere," he wrote, "for he realizes that to write only what he believes is to confess his narrowness and inflexible limitations. Perfectly sincere men have been or are rarely artists." [103] And when he added that by putting a premium on sincerity we are pledging ourselves to praise every sincere effort of the "intellectual slop merchants," however moronic, he provided us with an important key to his stand on the subject. Another key is the waggishness of the man himself.

One need read only a few pages of him to realize that he is not always sincere in what he writes, and that he was not wholly sincere in eulogizing insincerity.

[102] *Ibid.,* p. 622.
[103] *Another Book on the Theatre,* p. 59.

77

THE TRAGIC AND THE COMIC MUSE.—"Great drama, like great men and women, is always just a little sad," he wrote in a more sober moment. "Only idiots may be completely happy. Reflection, sympathy, wisdom, gallant gentleness, experience—the chords upon which great drama is played—these are wistful chords." [104]

But it does not follow that a sad play, a play which moves its audience to tears, is necessarily a serious play, or that a play which moves to frequent laughter is mere "good fun" and therefore less important than a tragedy. Nathan is himself once more, pointing out clear-eyed that art "is just as often gay as dour, just as often frothy as founded in stone"; [105] that "emotion and calm hard thinking seldom go together"; that the sentimentalist who confuses sad drama and serious drama fails to realize that often the play which puddles his eyes is sad "in proportion to its absence of thought"; [106] that life is still—as Walpole observed—a tragedy to those who feel and a comedy to those who think.

To write a truly great comedy, Nathan believes, calls for a wider cultural background and a finer skill than to write a great tragedy. Or, to borrow his own example and his terminology, a second-rate man could write *The Mar-*

104 *The Critic and the Drama*, p. 31.
105 *The Theatre, the Drama, the Girls*, p. 261.
106 *Another Book on the Theatre*, p. 76.

78

quis de Priola, but only a first-rate man could give us
Anatol.

> In comedy, . . . we find most of the true, deep,
> biting intelligence that has come down to us
> throughout the history of the drama. Comedy has
> made the human race wise, whereas drama has
> made it but merciful. It is comedy that has purged
> men of their delusions, whereas drama has only
> furthered and supported them. Aristophanes
> made his fellow-countrymen salubriously cogni-
> zant of their affectations, shams and hypocrisies;
> so Molière made his; so Shaw makes his today.
> The Greeks profited vastly more from the purga-
> tive humor of their comic writers than from the
> blood and agony of their tragic.[107]

And beyond these benefits we must not lose sight of
the fact that the theatre, after all, is "one of the world's
pleasures"—first, last, and always a toy—"something for
grown men to play with when the mood of seriousness is
not too heavy upon them . . ." [108]

"OUTHOUSE OF THE ARTS."—The legitimate
theatre may be the house of Satan, but the distinction of

[107] *Land of the Pilgrims' Pride,* p. 212.
[108] *The House of Satan,* p. 230.

being the outhouse of the arts Nathan grants only to the motion picture theatre. His attacks on the motion picture cover such a wide span of years and so many pages in so many volumes that, although we give them last place in our discussion, we cannot afford wholly to overlook them.

Criticizing the motion picture as "the result of a circumspect elimination of the principal attributes of four of the arts and a clever synthesis of the scum," [109] he pointed out that from literature the motion picture originally eliminated style; from drama, speech; from painting, color; and from sculpture, form and the third dimension. Since 1918, speech and color have been added to the motion picture, and now reports reach us that the third dimension may be the next step. Nathan acknowledges the advancement of the motion picture industry, but steadfastly continues to regard the cinema as trivial entertainment. In 1918 or 1919 he occasionally could work up a mild degree of interest in certain lighter aspects of the movies. Today that interest is totally lacking.

Let it be clearly understood that Nathan has never expressed the slightest interest in the cinema as an art or in its productions as a whole. He did bestow some favor long ago on Charlie Chaplin and on the comic movie. In 1919 he wrote, "Chaplin now and again is a serviceable diversion against the labored unfunniness of the posturing artists of Broadway." He praised Mack Sennett, who,

[109] *The Popular Theatre,* p. 129.

he noted, "is probably the most fecund inventor and merchant of the slapstick masque the civilized world has yet seen. . . . He has made probably twice as many millions laugh as have all Shakespeare's clowns and all the music show comedians on earth rolled together." And laughter, he added significantly, "knows no caste, no altitude of brow." [110] In his praise of slapstick movies he went all the way, pointing out that they displayed imagination, genuine comedy, knowledge of human nature, and that "as broad vulgar low comedy, they are not only superior to much of the vulgar low comedy of such as Shakespeare, but to the bulk of the low comedy of the modern theatre." [111]

And there his encomium abruptly ended. Low comedy. Unimportant entertainment. That is the place he grants to motion pictures, a place which they share—in his opinion—with "dime novels, vaudeville shows, cabaret music, billiards, and the free lunch." But as a serious competitor of serious drama, art of the ages, this twentieth century offshoot is merely ridiculous—"of unwitting ignorance, illiteracy, and stupidity all compact."

In 1921, several years after his self-dated reference to dime novels, vaudeville shows and the free lunch, he was chiefly concerned with the cinema—that "thundering flood of bilge and scum"—because movie magnates

[110] *Comedians All*, p. 200.
[111] *The Popular Theatre*, p. 129.

("maggots") were buying in Broadway theatre after Broadway theatre, and the future of American drama lay precariously in none too gentle hands. Still later, in 1926, his concern was with public taste. "The movies, nine hundred and ninety-nine out of every thousand of which are the veriest dramatic ditchwater, have slowly drowned the dramatic taste of the nation until today all that is left of it is a gurgle and a few bubbles." [112]

In a more detailed treatment of the shortcomings of motion pictures two years later, Nathan stressed the necessity for: (1) divorcing the business end from the producing end of the motion picture industry, (2) developing its own possibilities and not relying so heavily on stage drama, and (3) learning the limitations of the screen and abiding by them. Here he observed, too, that pictures are designed for a sort of least common denominator; that inasmuch as there "are no different circuits of movie houses, as there are in the case of theatres," [113] each picture must strive for mob appeal. "In the theatre," he added significantly, "things are different."

By 1931, even though talking pictures meanwhile had arrived and firmly entrenched themselves, Nathan's qualms had left him. Talking pictures, he predicted, would have no more effect on the legitimate theatre than silent movies had had, for the appeal of silent and talking movies

[112] *The House of Satan*, pp. 244–45.
[113] *Art of the Night*, p. 128.

alike was to "that very considerable portion of the public whose intelligence was not up to the strain imposed upon it by the theatre in general." [114] With this unstartling prognostication off his chest, he ventured a more startling prediction.

> A half dozen years ago, I wrote that the moving pictures would not last, that it was ridiculous to use the word art in connection with them, and that they would soon or late pass into limbo. The statement was jeered and I was set down a fool. Where is the old moving picture today? It is as dead as a doornail; it has disappeared from the scene almost completely. Emboldened, therefore, I make another prediction that will doubtless meet with the same derogation of my clairvoyant gifts. It is this: that the talkies will sooner or later go the way of the silent movies. . . . They will not overlong satisfy audiences, for all their relatively cheap admission prices, for audiences, low or high, have a way of disliking any substitutes for any real thing. [115]

Undeterred by the dubious reception given his prophecy by hinterlanders who have little opportunity to see

[114] *Testament of a Critic*, p. 199.
[115] *Ibid.*, p. 212.

the real thing and who hesitate to term the old moving picture dead as a doornail because it has undergone speech improvements, Nathan continues to feel encouraged about the whole situation. He even comments on two important contributions which Hollywood has made to Broadway. First, the talkies have drawn from the theatre the scum and the driftwood, and have left a higher type of audience which will respond to a higher type of drama. Secondly, Hollywood, in its eagerness to film the better dramas, has paid New York producers—he gives us an approximate figure—"annual sums running into hundreds of thousands of dollars for the mere screen rights to such plays as *Dead End, Pride and Prejudice, Winterset, Ethan Frome* . . ." [116] Thus obliquely Hollywood helps to foot the bill for many a Broadway play, at the same time financing, in a way, production of the better type of drama.

That the Hollywood versions of these Broadway plays are drama Nathan continues to doubt. Here are a few of his reasons. Moving pictures simply do not live. "They are the drama of a machine age designed for the consumption of robots." [117] They cannot fully develop and shade their characters. The greatest actor is the man in the cutting room. The after-image is not of the movie as a whole but of a single actor or actress. And finally, the motion picture depends upon motion, and its art is limited accordingly.

[116] *The Theatre of the Moment,* p. 111.
[117] *The Intimate Notebooks of George Jean Nathan,* p. 181.

In *The Morning After the First Night,* published in 1938, he relates that he decided to take a trip out to Hollywood and get a "clinical whiff" of this reputed threat to the theatre. After two weeks spent in close examination, he reported his findings. "Hollywood impresses me as being ten million dollars' worth of intricate and highly ingenious machinery functioning elaborately to put skin on boloney."

SUMMARY OF FINDINGS.—Looking back, we find Nathan's views on drama epitomized in his broad-minded, high-minded definition of good drama as "anything that interests an intelligently emotional group of persons assembled together in an illuminated hall." His broad-mindedness is further reflected in his attitude toward rules and technique. The mass of dramaturgic rules—of which he recognizes very few—he considers principally as shackles over which great drama triumphs. Technique he subordinates, realizing its value but stressing the superior importance of skill and imagination. Themes likewise matter little, treatment much. As for propaganda and war plays, best results follow an interval of time which allows judgment to cool and mature. Dramatic propaganda, at best, is futile.

On the high-minded side, we find Nathan the aristocrat disposing of the movies as boloney; Nathan the sophisticate exploding the fable that tragedy is more serious and consequently less trivial than comedy; Nathan the paradoxical aesthete emphasizing the primary importance of the play, the secondary importance of its production. But Nathan the aristocrat, although he believes firmly in the aristocracy of drama, cannot ignore the element of democracy in the theatre. And Nathan the intellectual, accepting the platitude that plays are platitudinous, scoffs at attempts at intellectual drama. Vastly more important than appeal to the intellect is appeal to the emotions, he contends, for drama generically is emotion.

CHAPTER THREE

The Nathan Critical Credo:
The Art of Criticizing Drama

ON the theory that "art is not helped and developed so much by criticism as by criticism of criticism," [1] Nathan, while criticizing the theatre and the drama, has not hesitated to criticize other critics and to comment at length on the art of criticism and its various aspects, axioms, and principles.

"The healthiest promise of American criticism is the increasing criticism of criticism, observable in many quarters," he remarked in *Testament of a Critic*, and went on to say that twenty years earlier, when critics (the impolite Nathan excepted) squeamishly refrained from criticizing one another, critical nonsense was enthroned and critical stagnation ensued. "Today, all is changed—and for the better. . . . The bricks fly back and forth and the softheads are knocked out . . . If our criticism, literature

---

[1] *The Autobiography of an Attitude*, p. 161.

and drama have advanced, it has been these bricks that have been largely responsible." [2]

But Nathan, though he criticizes frequently in terms of flying bricks, defines criticism with considerably greater eloquence. On criticism in general:

> . . . beauty is a sleep-walker in the endless corridors of the wakeful world, uncertain, groping, and not a little strange. And criticism is its tender guide.[3]

Again:

> Criticism is the windows and chandeliers of art: it illuminates the enveloping darkness in which art might otherwise rest only vaguely discernible, and perhaps altogether unseen.[4]

And again:

> Criticism of the arts consists in an intellectualization of emotionalism.[5]

We begin to see that criticism represents something more than brickbats and bouquets to George Jean Nathan. That criticism is an art is one of his most familiar conten-

[2] *Testament of a Critic*, pp. 28–29.
[3] *The Critic and the Drama*, p. 3.
[4] *Ibid.*, p. 4.
[5] *The World in Falseface*, p. 20.

tions. Moreover, he tells us stoutly, criticism is the most aristocratic of the arts; and the sole concern of dramatic criticism is with drama as an art.

> The business of dramatic criticism has no more to do with the box-office than the business of sewer inspection has to do with art. The business of dramatic criticism is, very simply, with drama as an art and the moment it concerns itself with drama in any other way it ceases to be dramatic criticism.[6]

Though dramatic criticism is itself an art, concerned with another art, its internal processes are not to be confused with those of art. "The concern of art is with beauty; the concern of criticism is with truth. And truth and beauty, despite the Sunday School, are often strangers." [7] The business of criticism, then, is to state facts—not to convince and convert, but merely to state facts. All too often criticism overreaches itself, seeking to plumb thoroughly the work of an artist, to reason it out. This is not the duty of criticism. The duty of criticism, according to Nathan, is "to reconstruct a great work of art on a diminutive scale," a scale within the reach of eyes not capable of gazing on high, to reproduce, in so far as possible, "the

[6] *The House of Satan*, p. 93.
[7] *The Critic and the Drama*, p. 7.

full richness of the artist's emotional organ tones . . . on the cold cerebral xylophone that is criticism's deficient instrument. In the accomplishment of these aims, it is bound by no laws that art is not bound by. There is but one rule: there are no rules. Art laughs at locksmiths." [8]

There are no rules. . . . But we must not bewilder ourselves by taking Nathan too literally, for, in the same book, he tells us, "If art knows no rules, criticism knows no rules—or, at least, none save those that are obvious." [9]

If art knows no rules . . . We recall the advice, previously noted, which he offered the hypothetical young critic:

> Don't go too far with the idea that there are no rules in the case of drama. There happen, fortunately or unfortunately, to be a few. Bumptiously to deny the existence of all such rules is to make one's self out a ninny. There are certain rules. What there are not, are commandments. [10]

Lest we despair prematurely, out of the confusion rise two well-defined critical doctrines, doctrines which are fundamental Nathanism, doctrines which are the stone foundation for the shifting sands of his contradictory criti-

---

[8] *Ibid.*, p. 57.
[9] *Ibid.*, p. 23.
[10] *Art of the Night,* p. 15.

cism. The first of these is the belief that every work of art is an entity, a matter of individual expression, and that every critical essay likewise is an entity, a thing in itself, equally free of definitions. There is no single formula for art, and there is no one formula for criticism. There are, legitimately, as many kinds of criticism as there are works to be criticized.

The second of these doctrines is Nathan's standard of criticism, absurdly simple to state, considerably more difficult to apply, and tremendously important in its effect on American dramatic criticism and American drama. The only standard of criticism which he recognizes is the appraisal of a play "in terms of the finest exemplars in its own field." Or, in the event of a completely original play, that play shall be appraised "in terms of the author's success or failure in the achievement of his plan and intention." [11] In other words, Nathan believes that the only way to criticize drama—or any other art—is from the top down.

He realizes, of course, that the easiest and most convenient approach to the business of dramatic criticism is to review plays in terms of the local popular theatre: such and such a play compares favorably with such and such a play which closed last month at the theatre next door. On hearsay, he recommends this as an excellent method of providing oneself with cigars from managers at Christ-

[11] *The Intimate Notebooks of George Jean Nathan*, p. 136.

mas and with effusive "H'ya, Georgie, old boy?" 's from
playwrights. The second easiest and most convenient approach to dramatic criticism is to review plays in terms of
"the present world theatre and its functioning dramatists."
This procedure is somewhat harder on the critic and on
the plays. But Nathan is one of the professionally few
who criticize plays only from the point of view of "the
very highest and proudest standards of all drama in
a like category." He admits that, as he was haplessly created to see it, the only "justification for the trade of dramatic criticism" is to "criticize drama and not merely
apologize for it." [12] The critic who permits, and perhaps
even praises, inferior wares is not only lazy and stupid, he
is definitely harmful, for the endorsement of inferior wares
can only delay the day when the finer theatre will come
into its own.

Here, then, is the kernel of the Nathanian critical credo.
First, criticism is an art, and every work of art is unique,
unfettered by "commandments." Secondly, a play may
be measured truly by only one yardstick: the perfect example in its own field. Add to these precepts three warn-
ings: the realization that morals, being geographical, have
no place in artistic judgments; that production and acting
shall carry no weight in dramatic criticism, which is an
evaluation of the play itself; and that theatrical criticism,
which is concerned with the theatre of the moment, is not

[12] *The Morning After the First Night,* p. 64.

to be confused with dramatic criticism, which treats of drama as an art of the ages. Add these, and the Nathanian critical structure begins to assume definite form.

He has more to say—much more. Some of it is weighty, more of it is witty. Some of it is dramatic criticism, some theatrical. Scattered though they are through twenty-five volumes, the important canons and comments can be sifted out, grouped, and presented in a form which Nathan himself frequently employs.

QUALIFICATIONS OF A CRITIC.—In hoisting the standards for judging plays, Nathan simultaneously hoists the qualifications of the judges. To appraise a play in terms of the finest example of its type necessitates that the critic be thoroughly familiar with the best drama in every field; that his knowledge be intensive and extensive; that he be free from parochialism, the curse of the American critic; that he know the dramas of other tongues and other times, and can apply that knowledge to the presentations of the moment; that he be equally familiar with world criticism; and, above all, that he be able to recognize fine drama when he sees it.

A lapse almost as serious as the inability to recognize fine drama is the too common tendency to mistake the fraudulent for the genuine. Concerning many plays—and Nathan suggests *The Master, Papa,* and *A Texas Nightin-*

gale—a difference of opinion is understandable. But when three members of the New York Critics' Circle prefer *Idiot's Delight* to *Winterset*, he feels justified in commenting that, "The future historian of modern American drama will have to read much of modern American criticism with his fingers crossed if he wishes to derive a true picture of modern dramatic worth." [13]

The qualifications of a critic who hopes to judge drama by Nathan's standards are higher than the qualifications of a playwright.

> . . . to write a single piece of living, first-rate criticism of a first-rate play, a man must have within his grasp the sweep of all the literatures and all the traditions of all the stages of the world. This one piece of first-rate criticism must automatically be builded upon what remain of the man's findings from all the first-rate criticism that has gone before, and it must, if it would survive, be superior to such prevenient criticism. Any one may copy Brunetière and die the next day unknown. To live on, one must improve on him and advance him.
>
> Dramatic criticism, unlike dramatic composition, demands without exception a knowledge of all drama, all human nature. It may not, like drama, concern itself alone with an imaginative

[13] *The Theatre of the Moment*, p. 22.

or photographic unit; it must be all-embracing, all-comprehensive. The writing of a *Romeo and Juliet* requires a very great genius; but the writing of a criticism of a *Romeo and Juliet* that shall endure as the play endures requires clearly a greater genius still. . . . Dryden, by his own confession, found his critical *Essay of Dramatic Poesy* a vastly more difficult labor than his drama *All For Love.*[14]

Attempts to define the exact qualities that make a critic first-rate, Nathan found abortive. "Intelligence, culture, background, experience, sympathy, sensitiveness, originality," all these qualities become mere rubber-stamps when a man possessing few of them can fortuitously be a first-rate critic, and a man possessing all of them, a second-rate one. A deep knowledge of theatre and drama—knowledge that gives substance to the reviews of the Shaws and the Nathans—is vital, but insufficient. There must be understanding—understanding of the drama, but also of the theatre. Nathan has it. Shaw has it. William Archer had it not. Archer, as Nathan put it, "followed the gypsy caravan in a dress suit." [15] There must be understanding, then, and inner warmth. But sympathy is not essential. "Criticism is often most sympathetic when it is apparently most cruel." Furthermore, sympathy connotes sentiment, and

[14] *The Popular Theatre,* pp. 93–94.
[15] *The House of Satan,* p. 80.

95

a surgeon, as he points out, is not at his peak of efficiency when he operates on his own wife. So Nathan frowns on sympathy *before* the fact; but he endorses sympathy *after* the fact. To enter the theatre certain of a pleasant evening, he explains, is an uncritical attitude. But to leave the theatre in the cheerful certainty that one has had a good time, that is true critical sympathy.

Only the best equipped critic is worthy of his task under the Nathanian code.

JOURNALISTIC CRITICISM.—And what is the place of journalistic criticism in Nathan's critical code? First, we must ascertain the relative quality of American journalistic criticism, recognizing that it is far higher today than twenty or thirty years ago.

When Nathan entered the field of criticism, in 1905, the reviewer's first consideration was not of the theatre as art, nor even as entertainment; it was of the theatre as a business. That such and such a play stank was of small concern to the reviewer. What did matter was the fact that the malodorous drama played to thousands of dollars last week, and that a large advertisement in the critic's paper probably would continue to adorn those pages for weeks to come, by the grace of God and the professional reviewer. In this period of praise-or-shut-up criticism, it was not unusual for a newspaper reviewer to lose his job for daring to criticize unfavorably the production of a popular playwright or producer. What *was* unusual was a critic who would utter such blasphemy. (Nathan, you will recall, soon left newspaper reviewing and entered the magazine field.)

Slowly the situation improved, but in 1922, the editorial injunction to the reviewer was still: "If you can't praise, don't dispraise." And in 1926, Nathan described the general run of reviews in the New York newspapers as "an amalgam of hotel news, flirtations, genial backslappings, bread and butter letters and *quid pro quos* that calls itself dramatic criticism." [16]

The reasons for these genial backslappings were not far to seek. Allowing the business angle and a lack of critical taste on the part of most of the reviewers, two other factors entered. The average American critic, Nathan maintained, was deficient in "the art of penetrating faultfinding." He did not *want* to praise indiscriminately; he merely found it "easier to write gush than diatribe," to conceal his ignorance under the pretense of a generous good nature. "The art of the careful, honest and demolishing *coup de grâce* is an art calling, first, for an exhaustive knowledge of the subject under the microscope, secondly, for an original and sharply inventive analytical turn of mind, and thirdly, for a wit and power over words . . ." [17]

[16] *The House of Satan*, p. 91.
[17] *Comedians All*, p. 15.

That most critics found this so-called destructive criticism "a rooster too difficult of winging" and soon gave up even the attempt is obvious to anyone who bothers to reread the drama pages of the newspapers of the period.

But even Nathan, master demolisher, shunned the job of theatrical reviewing in the teens and twenties, claiming that his genius was "insufficient to master the technique" of making extended comment on utter balderdash. "I can say all I have to say about such plays in one word, and no newspaper in America would print the word." [18] In other words, when there is no drama, there can be no dramatic criticism. And the fault of the journalistic criticism of the first quarter of the century lay not alone with the reviewers but also with the newspapers' arbitrary policy of reviewing every theatrical presentation, however ignoble.

During the twenties the quality of American journalistic criticism took a sharp turn for the better, and this improved quality continues to mark the majority of dramatic reviews in the forties. Present-day reviewers are more intelligent, less prejudiced and parochial; present-day reviewers are often penetrating and helpful—with what result? The result, Nathan contends, is that the theatre is damaged. The theatre is damaged—not by dramatic criticism, however destructive—but by journalistic criticism, which persists in covering the entire range of theatrical offerings.

[18] *The House of Satan*, p. 89.

Nathan's argument against this policy of blanket coverage runs somewhat as follows. Of, say, the hundred and fifty plays presented in the legitimate theatres of New York City during a given season, the great majority are comparatively worthless. This is true even today, despite advances of the last decade. Dramatic criticism ignores these meretricious plays. But journalistic criticism, being of reportorial nature, must notice them, and, being of the improved, honest variety, must point out their deficiencies to the public. Week after week the public reads of "bad plays, dull plays, boresome plays, trashy plays, depressing plays." And the theatre suffers.

The theatre suffers, he explains, because it is an idiosyncrasy of the theatre-going public to regard the theatre as a whole, not as a series of distinct organizations and productions, but as *the* theatre. The percentage of trashy novels, bad paintings, sculpture, music, et cetera, in the average season likewise is great, he contends, but the public thinks of *a* novel, or *an* art gallery, and literature and painting are not seriously damaged.

In his *Intimate Notebooks*, published in 1932, Nathan proposes a "reconstitution" of the methods of play reviewing:

> Let this play reviewing be as honest and as forthright as it in general presently is, but let there be a clear and unmistakable segregation of its various

performances. . . . Under the heading of *The Theatre*, or *The Play*, let it review such exhibits as *Mourning Becomes Electra, The Barretts of Wimpole Street, The Left Bank, The Moon in the Yellow River* and, say, a dozen or so other such worthy or relatively worthy productions in the course of a season. And let it have some such heading as *Not the Theatre*, or *The Rubbish Heap*, or *The Ashcan*, or something of the sort for the twaddle that the theatre-in-name-only annually, even in its most prosperous times, uncovers. Thus will *the* theatre and mere buildings temporarily housing so-called plays . . . be clearly dissociated in the public's mind.

So long as the newspapers bunch theatres under a common head and bunch the plays in them under the common head of drama, just so long will the public be discouraged from theatrical attendance. . . . It is up to the newspapers and their reviewers to make it clear that certain structures that happen to have stages in them are not always necessarily part and parcel of the institution known as the theatre.[19]

To summarize, journalistic criticism, however well intended, errs in furthering the confusion of tawdry the-

[19] *The Intimate Notebooks of George Jean Nathan*, pp. 141–43.

atrical productions with the theatre. It errs in devoting space to inferior plays which warrant no consideration. Dealing by its very nature with the mass, with plays of every quality, reviewing for a mob that wants to know what to go to, not what to stay away from, it is ill-fitted for the scheme of criticism whose only standard is perfection.

DESTRUCTIVE CRITICISM.—That he is a destructive critic is Nathan's proudest and most frequent boast. He is destructive, not as the prelude to reform, but because it is his nature to pick to pieces, "to proclaim the flaw." Even Nathan himself is the victim of his attacks. His books are composed, he would have us believe, by a series of self-inflicted, figurative blows on the Nathan nose. An aesthetic sadist, he once found that a published book of his own failed to meet his critical demands, whereupon he sat down and wrote and printed (under a pseudonym) a criticism of the book and of himself, "the which perfectly just criticism, upon subsequent reading, impressed me as exceedingly harsh and unfriendly—if not, indeed, positively vicious," he added.[20]

This same harshness, this same apparent viciousness, appears again and again in Nathan's comments on the drama and the theatre. His reputation as an insulting fellow is firmly established. But his destructive criticism is

[20] *Mr. George Jean Nathan Presents*, p. 182.

less an indication of an irascible disposition than an indi-cation, instead, of high hopes and high standards, a re-fusal to compromise with mediocrity. Nor does he destroy in order that the playwright may rebuild a truer structure. He destroys what is inartistic because it is inartistic. De-structive? Constructive? Small matter. Both terms are misnomers.

It is Nathan's contention that American criticism is seriously damaged by the notion that so-called construc-tive criticism is valuable and that so-called destructive criticism is not. This conviction has resulted in reams of "architectonic advice" flowing from the pens of critics who lack the structural faculty; advice which, if it were followed, "would produce a drama twice as poor as that which they criticize." [21]

Again, constructive criticism is confused with the pat on the back, the kind of criticism that enthroned Augustus Thomas, Owen Davis, Charles Klein, and David Belasco.

> Paraphrasing Pascal, to little minds all things are great. . . . The little mind and its little criti-cism are the flattering foes of sound art. Such art demands for its training and triumph the count-less preliminary body blows of muscular criticism guided by a muscular mind. Art and the artist can-not be developed by mere back-slapping.[22]

[21] *The Critic and the Drama*, p. 125.
[22] *Ibid.*, pp. 9–10.

This muscular criticism guided by a muscular mind is the widely disparaged destructive criticism. If destructive criticism is criticism that pulls down without building up, Nathan observes, then three-fourths of the best dramatic criticism of the last three hundred years is worthless. But destructive criticism, in pulling down, clears the way for advancement. In tipping over the "cheap gilt thrones" of the George Broadhursts and David Belascos of yesterday, destructive criticism cleared the decks for the vastly more reputable American drama of today. And the process is continuous.

To this defense of destructive criticism, the frequent response is, "Any fool can find fault." That any fool can find fault, Nathan grants. But the ability to find fault accurately, soundly, and searchingly he labels a decidedly uncommon talent. "He who can, does; he who can't, criticizes," is the next quoted recrimination. Nathan replies with the names of four contemporaries who "can" and who criticize—Bernard Shaw, William Archer, Ashley Dukes, and St. John Ervine—and with the contention that dramatic criticism is an art more difficult to master than the art of drama. And finally, he throws a hearty challenge to the hypothetical young critic:

> Don't be afraid of being labeled a destructive critic. You will be in good company. Where would you rather be: in Hell with Swift, Voltaire and

103

Nietzsche or in the American Institute of Arts and Letters with Richard Burton, Clayton Hamilton and Hermann Hagedorn? [23]

THE PREJUDICED CRITIC.—Producers frequently expect critics to approach a dramatic exhibit "with a mind purged of all prejudice." This is possible, Nathan grants —but only when the critic is a complete blockhead. Every man of any intelligence, every man capable of profiting by experience and education, has derived therefrom certain prejudices. The critic who is without prejudice is without viewpoint, "unfit for his job, . . . a strayed buffoon."

In his advice to that same young critic, Nathan urges him to give free course to his violent prejudices, however unorthodox, only being careful to avoid indignation and "always to smile." (The smile is a precautionary device; if the critic is wrong, the general public will conclude that he was just fooling.)

But there is another side to the story, another form of prejudice. Too many critics play favorites. The critic sets his pet upon a pedestal and strives to keep him there. Disappointing new work by the favorite reflects on the critic's judgment, or so the critic sometimes reasons, and consequently he praises or ignores plays he should condemn.

[23] *Art of the Night*, p. 9.

ART OF CRITICIZING DRAMA

"The bulk of American criticism," Nathan believes, "is corrupted by a blind adherence to and championing of favorites." [24]

Blending these two observations, we find, not surprisingly, that ideally the intelligent man is "out of the very necessity of his intelligence a bundle of presumptions and predilections," but, at the same time, his mind is open to new ideas, new philosophies, new convictions . . . In short, his prejudices are pliable.

PERSONAL CRITICISM.—Another familiar contention is that dramatic criticism must be aloof, detached, impersonal. To this, Nathan replies, "Criticism is personal, or it is nothing." The impersonal critic is a mere reporter. Of all critics, the dramatic critic is the most intensely personal.

> Drama is a two-souled art: half divine, half clownish. Shakespeare is the greatest dramatist who ever lived because he alone, of all dramatists, most accurately sensed the mongrel nature of his art. Criticism of drama, it follows, is similarly a two-souled art: half sober, half mad. . . . This is why the best criticism of the theatre must inevitably be

[24] *Ibid.*, p. 13.

personal criticism. The theatre itself is distinctly personal; its address is directly personal.[25]

Dramatic criticism, then, is personal because drama is personal. It is personal, furthermore, because it must take into consideration the personality of the dramatist. "Show me how I can soundly criticize the drama of Wedekind without analyzing Wedekind, the man . . ." [26] Of what value is criticism of a play by Strindberg that fails to consider that Strindberg "personally was a lunatic"?—or of a play by Pinero, treating of English characters, which fails to consider that Pinero was "of ineradicable Portuguese mind and blood"? And finally, dramatic criticism is personal, because it is "the critic's art of appraising himself in terms of various forms of drama." [27] Criticism is autobiography; it is the man.

Criticism impersonal? "Talk to me of impersonal criticism," Nathan replies, "and I'll talk to you of impersonal sitz-bathing." [28]

THE CRITIC'S NIGHT OFF.—Fifteen years or so ago, when he was visiting in London, Nathan was entertained at a dinner given in his honor by the distinguished

[25] *The Critic and the Drama*, pp. 20–21.
[26] *Ibid.*, p. 144.
[27] *Ibid.*, p. 118.
[28] *Ibid.*, p. 143.

dramatic critics, William Archer and Arthur Bingham Walkley. An illustrious group of British critics and theatrical personages were present, he relates, and in due time he was called on for a speech. He rose and began solemnly, "The recent tendency in American drama—"

"The hell with the recent tendency in American drama!" howled Archer and Walkley. "What we want to hear about is the Ziegfeld *Follies!*" [29]

And so it is with critics—and not with critics alone. Any man who appreciates fine art appreciates, too, an occasional "artistic sabbath," as Nathan frequently has pointed out. Eugene O'Neill devours detective and mystery novels—Nathan sets the figure at six or seven a week. George Bernard Shaw confessed years ago to an inordinate enjoyment of Harold Lloyd moving pictures. Thomas Hardy, on his rare visits to London, invariably selected a music hall show where he could see "one droll swat another across the beak. . ." And James Huneker, dean of New York critics of a generation ago, "used to sneak out of the Metropolitan in the middle of *Tannhäuser* and gallop down the block to the theatre where George Bickel was doing his fiddle-tuning act." [30]

It is not surprising, then, to learn that the serious dramatic critics, men who venerate fine drama, also go on an occasional "Gothic spree." The late William Archer,

[29] *Encyclopaedia of the Theatre,* p. 274.
[30] *The House of Satan,* p. 60.

model of decorum, confessed to Nathan a preference for Florence Mills and her colored hoofers; and the late A. B. Walkley, admitting that he found Ibsen a little too grim, too hyperborean, announced that the *Follies* were infinitely more to his taste. Brooks Atkinson, erudite critic for the New York *Times*, roars with laughter at the antics of Bert Lahr and Jack Haley. And Nathan himself likes low burlesque shows and strip-tease artistes, particularly Chinese,[31] calls himself a pushover for the tricks of professional prestidigitators and stage magicians, and has been in regular attendance at the circus—surely not always in the line of duty—since his papa had to hold the bottle of pop to George Jean's mouth so it wouldn't drip over his lace collar. "The wittiest line of Alfred Capus," he acknowledges, "makes me laugh in the theatre not one-tenth so hard as the spectacle of one pickle-herring clouting another over the ear with a chocolate éclair, but do I admit the fact? I do not. And why?" [32]

Why? The answer projects us abruptly into another phase of our discussion, the criticism of laughter.

ON LAUGHTER.—Joseph Wood Krutch, drama critic for *The Nation*, in his 1937 mid-season digest of plays

[31] For a learned critical discussion of the strip-tease, burlesque, musical shows, the radio soap opera, the circus, cabarets, carnival shows, and Coney Island, see Nathan's *The Entertainment of a Nation* (1942).

[32] *The Popular Theatre*, pp. 226–27.

saw fit to recommend twelve current productions. Of these twelve, Nathan points out, Mr. Krutch recommended ten on the ground that they were funny—"exciting and funny . . . some good gags . . . irresistibly funny . . . amusing . . ."

Now Nathan, as we have observed, likes a good laugh-show. And he doesn't turn up his nose at a belly-laugh, for he believes that "any man who discriminates between two hearty laughs is idiotic . . ." and that the aforementioned fiddle-tuning act "is not less art of its sort than the most comical line in Beaumarchais." [33]

But Nathan does believe that the future of the American theatre is imperiled by too much critical stress on laughter. The laugh-show enjoys a nine-stroke critical advantage over the more serious play of equal quality. And playwrights, quick to sense the fact, are striving for laughter—at the expense of more important dramatic matters.

> Laughter is surely no thing to be slighted . . . But a stage that caters to it at the expense of so much else and a general public that venerates it theatrically above all else can never in combination hope for a theatre much above grade B. That is the threatening weakness of our immediate American theatre.[34]

[33] *The World in Falseface*, p. 67.
[34] *The Morning After the First Night*, p. 50.

And the burden, he seems to feel, lies upon the critics.

CRITICAL HONESTY.—Laughter, light drama, the relative enjoyment which a critic derives from pleasant dramatic trivia and a somber classic, each of these topics leads in turn to the matter of critical honesty. All criticism, Nathan once said, is a lie. The dramatic critic, like the lawyer defending a guilty client, best serves his purpose as a convincing liar. "He must, for the good of the theatre, deny with all the vouchers and eloquence at his command that the theatre is a mere place for light amusement." [35]

The "well-educated, well-bred, well-fed man" may go to the theatre for relief from his steady diet of fine literature and profound thought, for "diversion by contrast" —in the form of "horse-play, belly laughter, . . . insane melodrama, lovely limbs, . . . gaudy colours . . ." But these diversions, he tells us, are fit for only the highest type of theatregoer. The average theatregoer

> is under-educated and under-bred and thus not aesthetically ready for the custard-pie arts which are meet for his well-educated and well-bred brother. . . . And so, gentlemen, when I write in the public prints that I enjoy the comedy of

[35] *The Popular Theatre*, p. 227.

Shakespeare more than the comedy of Harry Watson, Jr., I lie. . . . My only apology is that I lie, and nobly, for the good of the theatre.[36]

This is not Nathan's only argument against critical veracity. Elsewhere he refers to honesty as the leading fault of American criticism, and goes on to say that

There is altogether too much honesty. The greater the blockhead, the more honest he is. And as a consequence the criticism of these blockheads, founded upon their honest convictions, is worthless.[37]

Here, in striving for effect, he has partly buried his meaning. Nine years later he tried again, with greater success.

Honesty of opinion is not unusual in American critical writing. The weakness of much of that writing lies in its failure to combine the honesty of opinion with basically sound judgment.[38]

In other words, opinions honestly expressed are worthless if these opinions are based on ignorance or on unsound

[36] *Ibid.*, pp. 233–34.
[37] *The Critic and the Drama*, p. 115.
[38] *Testament of a Critic*, p. 31.

judgment. The fault, then, lies with the opinion, not with its honesty.

Thus far we find honesty in criticism undesirable in two instances: first, when it necessitates eulogizing trivialities, however pleasant the critics may have found them, and secondly, when the convictions thus honestly expressed were better not expressed at all.

But just how prevalent *is* critical honesty? "I have capitalized honesty," Nathan once said. "It has been a profitable business. I have had little competition in the field of dramatic criticism, so the job has been an absurdly simple one." [39] Match this against his comment of the same period, that "there is altogether too much honesty" in criticism, and what have we? We are left with our tongues in our cheeks and a firm belief in Nathan's relish for paradox. And we doff our hats in profound admiration that each new contradiction, as he sets it before us, seems grounded in reason.

Somewhere between the problems of critical truth and critical untruth must lie the half-truths of criticism. The homely saying that the half-truth, like the half brick, carries farther was not lost on Nathan, who has sprinkled half-truths generously through his volumes, particularly the earlier ones. But he does not champion this sacrifice of truth.

[39] Goldberg, *The Theatre of George Jean Nathan,* p. 97.

These half-truths serve criticism as sauce serves asparagus: they give tang to what is otherwise often tasteless food. This is particularly true with criticism at its most geometrical and profound, since such criticism, save in rare instances, is not especially lively reading. But, nevertheless, the sauce is not the asparagus.[40]

Here we follow our labyrinthian topic of critical honesty around another turn. Nathan denies that he is always truthful, pointing out that he is "not ass enough to pretend to know absolutely what the truth is." [41] He does try to write what he believes is the truth, he adds, and, as far as he knows, he does so without ulterior motives, with no bone to pick. But "thoroughly honest and uninfluenced criticism is possible only to a critic who lives alone on top of an Alp." [42]

It is impossible for any man, save he be a disgusting boor, not to be influenced by charming personal friendships, by invitations to agreeable parties, by adroitly maneuvered and convincingly propelled flattery, by gifts of schnapps and fancy lead pencils. . . . Some of us are given to the

[40] *The Critic and the Drama,* pp. 75–76.
[41] *The World in Falseface,* p. 154.
[42] *The Autobiography of an Attitude,* p. 173.

pose that such things mean absolutely nothing to us, that we are not so absurdly to be hornswoggled from the path of duty and the pursuit of truth, but we know in our hearts that we are lying. Show me the critic who can go to a series of parties at a playwright's house, smoke the playwright's toothsome segars, drink the playwright's tasty liquor, and eat the playwright's wife's palatable Welsh rabbits—my own invitations, as I have said, doubtless went astray; the mails are getting *very* careless—and then write that the plays of the playwright are the flubdub they actually are . . . All that I can say is that I could not do it, and I am notoriously an evil-mannered, self-centered and pertinaciously nasty fellow, answerable only to God and the police.[43]

THE COWARDLY CRITIC.—The relation between a critic's courage and the integrity of his criticism is obvious. "It took more nerve and downright courage to write the *Essay on Morals* than it took to fight the battle of Waterloo," [44] Nathan observed.

American criticism today is a far cry from the praise-or-shut-up criticism of thirty years ago. Most of the criti-

[43] *The World in Falseface*, pp. 214–15.
[44] *Art of the Night*, p. 8.

cism we read today, Nathan believes, is fundamentally honest. But even now it scrupulously refrains from revealing the whole truth. Few American critics have the courage to refer, for example, to the disgusting effeminacy of many English actors, to the hideous, sagging antiquity of certain American leading ladies, to the fact that performances have been ruined because the leading player was drunk, etc., etc. "Each time," Nathan points out, the critics "have quibbled and have cheated the truth." Theatrical criticism "betrays itself when it substitutes euphemisms for what is unhappily true and objectionable." [45] This is particularly noticeable when the criticism treats of the deceased. "Simply because God in His infinite wisdom has seen fit to call Belasco away from the American theatre, the commentators . . . are given to an excessive civility whenever they are brought to mention his name." [46] But not Nathan. As he once remarked of William Winter, "The fact that Winter is dead doesn't increase my respect for him in the slightest." [47]

Most of this concerns theatrical criticism, but it may be applied equally to dramatic criticism. Criticism, theatrical or dramatic, demands courage. More than that, it demands a measure of boorishness. A man who "avoids

---

[45] *The Morning After the First Night*, p. 7.
[46] *Ibid.*, p. 8.
[47] *Comedians All*, p. 255.

offense against punctilio, . . . who is ready to sacrifice the truth to good manners and good form, and who has respect and sympathy for the feelings of his inferiors" [48] may be a gentleman, but he is no critic.

The desire for personal popularity also figures in this problem of critical courage and honest criticism. The American critic is still too fond of being on the popular side to be completely courageous in voicing unpopular opinions.

> He is fearful of his position in the community, of his neighbor's opinion, of the opinion of his potential prospective employers, of what will be thought of him tomorrow by someone whom he doesn't know today. I know whereof I speak. I am an American critic. And I had to fight with myself long years before I achieved my present—and even still but comparative—integrity. [49]

To Nathan's "even still but comparative integrity" universal tribute is paid. Typical are the comments of St. John Ervine, British playwright and critic, who remarked aptly, "He is not one of those persons who will scratch your back if you will scratch his," [50] and of the

[48] *The World in Falseface*, p. 39.
[49] *Ibid.*, p. 40.
[50] Ervine, St. John, "Ervine on Nathan," *The Living Age*, CCCXL (May, 1931), 306.

late Arnold Daly, outstanding American actor, who wrote, "Strangely enough, it is not Nathan's ability, brilliancy, or knowledge that impresses one most—it is his courage." [51]

THE COCKSURE CRITIC.—The critic who would sell his wares must call them loud and confidently. But those opinions which he ballyhoos so lustily must first have been whetted by doubts and kneaded into shape by qualifications.

Five bits from Nathan cover his views on the subject adequately.

> Criticism, above every other craft in the modern world, save alone politics and commercial theology, is a matter of steadily loud assurance. Much of American dramatic criticism, unlike some of that in England, enjoys the steady loudness, but it lacks the necessary underlying assurance, or at least the convincing air of assurance.[52]

> It is the first duty and mark of the successful critic to be as sure of himself in public as he is now and then unsure of himself in private.[53]

[51] Daly, Arnold, "On George Jean Nathan—and Perhaps Some Other Critics" *The Bookman*, LIII (Apr., 1921), 163.
[52] *Passing Judgments*, p. 142.
[53] *Ibid.*, p. 6.

The cocksure critic may sometimes be an ass, but at least he is always more readable than the perhaps sounder critic given to hesitations, doubts, and qualifications. It may be too bad, but it is, alas, true.[54]

As I grow older, I notice that the word "perhaps" begins to appear more and more often in my critical writings. I am perhaps not so sure of the truth of what I believe as I once was.[55]

Criticism is the prevailing of intelligent skepticism over vague and befuddled prejudice and uncertainty. It answers no riddle: it merely poses an oppugnant and contradictory riddle. When the critic ceases to have self-doubts, he ceases to be a critic and becomes a pedagogue.[56]

ON CONTRADICTIONS.—Nathan's criticism has been said to "squirm" with contradictions. It would be hard to find a word more apt. One who sets for himself the task of reading all of Nathan's critical works, and distilling, bottling and labeling his opinions, frequently faces

[54] *Ibid.*, p. 4.
[55] *The Autobiography of an Attitude*, p. 19.
[56] *Materia Critica*, p. 3.

a web of contradictions. Before he is half through *Passing Judgments*, he may decide that Nathan's judgments are indeed passing. He learns to expect self-contradictions from this man who finds intense joy in contradicting others. In viewing his criticism as a whole, however, the reader is likely to find that the surface ripples are only the outward manifestations of a deep-running current which flows steadily in one direction. Drama, to Nathan, is movement and progress and change. Criticism, if it hopes to mirror drama, also must change, and thereby appears to contradict itself. "Beware of the critic who does not now and then contradict himself. He is a foe of the progress and development of art." [57]

Certainly Nathan's inconsistencies reveal no lack of honesty or sincerity. They reveal, instead, an ability to see several sides of a question and a desire to express altered opinions as enthusiastically, as honestly, as sincerely as he expressed the opinions which they contradict. Perhaps the best explanation of many of his contradictions is that he himself many times has gone to extremes in waging war on extreme fashions in the theatre. Allowance must be made for the methods of a fighting critic who at all times has his eye on the conditions of an actual drama and theatre.

Paradoxically, Nathan is superbly consistent on this subject of critical inconsistencies. The happiest statement

[57] *The World in Falseface*, p. 23.

of his stand is this paragraph from his first book, published in 1915.

> The best critics are the inconsistent critics.
> Show me a consistent critic, a critic who sets him-
> self a critical creed and abides by that creed with
> never a sidestep, never a whispered doubt, and I
> will show you a critic who is generally wrong. The
> theatre and its drama are as inconsistent institu-
> tions as the surface of the earthly sphere reveals.
> Dramatic criticism, if definitively and regularly
> consistent, becomes, therefore, as proportionately
> unsound as a brief on nose troubles written
> twenty-five years ago.[58]

GREAT DRAMA AND GREAT CRITICISM.—On
the relation between great drama and great criticism Nathan's comments have varied widely.

A. *Where there is no art, there is no call for criticism.*[59] Nathan contended—specifically, in 1917 and
1931—that this platitude warrants repetition, that negligible drama provides criticism "no soil in which it may
develop and grow"; that contemptible drama, although
it is easy to criticize amusingly, is "the greatest foe of

[58] *Another Book on the Theatre*, p. 307.
[59] *Mr. George Jean Nathan Presents*, p. 173.

120

criticism itself"; and that "behind every really great dramatic critic you will find one or more great dramatists." [60]

B. *Great criticism often from little acorns grows*—one
of the smaller acorns being the "third-rate preface to his
brother-in-law's book of fourth-rate plays" from which
grew the oak that is Dryden's *Defense of an Essay of
Dramatic Poesy.* Nor is this an isolated instance. Some
of Lessing's best criticism, Nathan shows us, "grew out
of completely negligible theatrical performances. And
Goethe wrote imperishable criticism that grew out of
plays by Kotzebue, Raupach and Iffland . . ." [61]

Thus Nathan stood on the subject in the early twenties, and as the twenties drew to a close he reviewed and
confirmed his opinion.

> If, from time to time in the course of my criti-
> cal activities, I select for discussion trivial plays
> which reach the storehouse before the words on
> them reach my readers, it is because now and then
> I find in them certain elements that suggest the
> bases for general critical doctrines. The perfect
> play, after all, offers small ground for interesting
> critical exploration . . . for all the things that
> may be said of perfect plays have already been
> said a hundred times and said better than anyone

[60] *Testament of a Critic,* pp. 29–30.
[61] *The World in Falseface,* p. xix.

presently performing in the critical pulpit, myself
surely included, can say them. . . . And nothing
has been said of the finest work produced in our
time that hasn't been a mere cuckooing of what
was written of the finest work of other times by
the critics of other days.

. . . The point is simply that, since we know
what absolute worth is . . . the business of criticism has become the business not so much of arguing that what is excellent is excellent as of
arguing that what is not excellent should be excellent, and trying to indicate, as best it can, the ways
and means gradually to make it so. Criticism, otherwise, is of small service and is converted into a
mere parlor game of slap-hands . . .

Many of the most valuable contributions to
dramatic criticism have been inspired by negligible dramatic and poetical works; many of the least
valuable by modern critics who, laboring under
the delusion of professional dignity, have sought
to plough up already long ploughed-up classical
ground.[62]

Perhaps we are to infer that the acorn may be smallish
but not infinitesimal; that, although a dwarf acorn dwarfs
the oak, nevertheless—and here our metaphor deserts us

[62] *Art of the Night*, pp. 218–23.

—a moderately good play lends itself better to criticism than a play which is above reproach.

But there stands some of Lessing's best criticism, by-product of "completely negligible theatrical performances."

ACTOR-RIDDEN CRITICISM.—The purpose of dramatic criticism is to criticize drama. To criticize the actors of that drama is to confuse the issue. Twenty-nine years ago Nathan bared the American critical subterfuge of concealing a total lack of understanding of Ibsen plays by confining the remarks solely to the acting. In 1926 his gibes were directed at critics who were "hornswoggled" by plays which "permit the star to let loose with histrionic hell"—violent overacting akin to "the throes of peripheral epilepsy." [63] And today, and always, he urges that critical emphasis fall upon the drama. Speaking for himself, he says that "nothing much seems critically to matter save the play itself, that is, the artist's work uncorrupted by the parasitic art that has been laid over it." [64]

In England, he points out, the players are of first importance; in America, the plays. And he adds that the present vitality of the American theatre—and lethargy of the British—may be traced to this source.

[63] *The House of Satan*, p. 40.
[64] *The Intimate Notebooks of George Jean Nathan*, p. 144.

GEORGE JEAN NATHAN

In America we went through a process of actor
veneration similar to that of the English for a
period of thirty years, and in that period the outstanding native plays were . . . abysmal drool.
. . . With less attention paid to the actor and
more to the dramatist, a finer species of drama
has been encouraged. . . . That we have a long
and hard way yet to go is plainly obvious, but at
least the strides strike me as being in the right
critical direction.[65]

THE PLACE OF EMOTIONS.—"Dramatic criticism
at its best," Nathan once observed, "is the adventure of
an intelligence among the emotions." Here a key word requires definition. "Intelligence," Nathan specified, "is
made up, in large part, of dead emotions; ignorance, of
emotions that have lived on, deaf and dumb and crip-
pled, but ever smiling." Consequently, Nathan takes issue with those theories of dramatic criticism which hold
that a critic must know thoroughly the technicalities of
drama and production but may be emotionally ignorant.
A judge who has never been in jail may judge wisely, he
points out; likewise, a critic may capably criticize the depiction of emotions he has never experienced, "but that
critic is nevertheless the most competent whose emotions

[65] *Ibid.*, p. 250.

124

the dramatis personæ do not so much anticipatorily stir up as recollectively soothe." [66]

The insight of emotions experienced adds tremendously to the competence—not to mention the readability—of Nathan's dramatic criticism.

WRITING THE REVIEW.—Nathan's comments on the composition of the critical essay, like his comments on drama and criticism in general, presuppose that his reader has a thorough grasp of the fundamentals. Progressing from that point, we find him reiterating that he does not believe in any one theory of criticism or any one formula for its composition; that criticism may take as many forms as the drama criticized, being at times tragic or melodramatic, at other times comic, farcical, or burlesque; that it may be constructive or destructive, emotional or cerebral, analytical or impressionistic with equal soundness, depending on the critic and the drama.

Nathan's remarks grouped under this catchall heading, then, are largely miscellaneous. First he warns critics to avoid enthusiasms, which he terms the endowment of immaturity. "The sound critic is not a cheer leader, but a referee. Art is hot, criticism cold." [67]

Though criticism is cold, the critic is "full of warmth," but "he suggests the presence of the heat within him

[66] *The Critic and the Drama*, pp. 133–34.
[67] *Ibid.*, p. 117.

without radiating it. This inner warmth is essential to a critic." [68]

As enthusiasm is to be avoided, so the critic must shun sentimentality, scourge of the American critical clan, whose calendar year "contains three hundred and sixty-five Valentine Days," [69] and indignation, "the seducer of thought." Here he adds a note of reservation. "There is an indignation that springs from the head and an indignation that springs from the heart. . . . My feelings are never indignant; my mind occasionally is." [70]

And all the while the critic must remember that his readers regard him as they regard a physician—as one whose professional knowledge is profound but whose advice is unpalatable. So Nathan urges the critic to "cajole" his patients by developing a "critical bedside manner" which cloaks his knowledge in humor and modesty. Fifteen years earlier he proffered the same advice in somewhat different terms. ". . . hard logic, stripped to the buff, can accomplish nothing. What the mass of the public wants is not constructive evidence, tough facts and straight-line reasoning, but evidential sky-rockets, pinwheels and flower-pots." [71] And Nathan gives it to them.

He gives it to them in flashing paradoxes and topsy-turvy reasoning, with ribald impudence and scholarly per-

[68] *Ibid.*, p. 8.
[69] *The World in Falseface*, p. 172.
[70] *The Autobiography of an Attitude*, p. 158.
[71] *Materia Critica*, p. 6.

ception, in torrents of criticism alternately pleonastic and
epigrammatic—more often, alas, the former. But primarily his pin-wheels and flower-pots are hearty American
slang, and his advice to a young critic includes a paragraph in its stout defense:

> Since you are an American, write like an Amer-
> ican. . . . Express yourself in the pungent idiom
> of your time, your land and your people; there is
> no apology necessary; that idiom may produce
> sound literature as well as the language of the
> dons. Don't be afraid of slang if it will make your
> point better and more forcibly than literose ex-
> pression. Much that was erstwhile slang has
> already been accepted into the dictionaries of for-
> mal English; much more will be accepted in the
> near future. The objection to slang, at least to
> the more valid slang, is snooty and snobbish.
> . . . But, on the other hand, don't make the
> mistake of believing that a mere imitation of
> Brook, Indiana, will get you any farther than an
> imitation of Cambridge, England.[72]

ONE-WORD REVIEWS.—Nathan himself has found
slang so effective that occasionally he can review an en-

[72] *Art of the Night*, pp. 9–10.

tire play in one word—"tripe!" And anyone who bothers to explain why tripe is tripe, in his opinion, is "not a critic so much as he is a pretentious and imbecile space-filler. . . . When a house has smallpox in it, the best and most sufficient thing to do is to tack a card on it reading *Smallpox*." [73]

HUMOR IN CRITICISM.—Nathan claims to have pasted on his office piano—"next to the rack of Beethoven's scherzi"—this from Voltaire:

> If Nature had not made us a little frivolous, we should be most wretched. It is because one can be frivolous that the majority do not hang themselves.

Voltaire's words assuage Nathan's feelings, he tells us, "when some nuisance invades my sanctum and deplores my occasional professional levity." [74]

Let us suppose that Nathan once saw fit to reply to such a nuisance and state his own case for humor in criticism. We can recreate the scene by assembling bits from half a dozen books, attributing to Nathan only his own words. The nuisance's part of the dialogue is not hard

[73] *Testament of a Critic*, p. 52.
[74] *The Intimate Notebooks of George Jean Nathan*, p. 165.

to imagine. Nathan gives us his guest's opening lines with the observation that "what the aforesaid nuisance observes is always of a cut."

> NUISANCE: Why do you, fundamentally a serious critic, so often spoil your reputation by indulging in facetiousness and buffoonery?

> NATHAN: There has seldom been a good critic who has not been deplored on the score of his frivolity. . . . Shaw . . . Leigh Hunt . . . George Henry Lewes . . . Hazlitt . . .[75] Our humorless college professors, third-rate authors, bad actors and magazine-cover artists who are constantly howling against humor in criticism— a humor that, to them, is synonymous with flippancy—will find, if they care to take the trouble, that fine art itself is often just as flippant as the criticism which they deride. In the midst of his finest tragedy, Shakespeare is periodically as flippant as Shaw is in the midst of his finest criticism.[76] There is a place for apt humor in even the most serious work. If there is a place for it in *Hamlet*, why shouldn't there be a place for it in a criticism of *Hamlet?* [77]

[75] *Ibid.,* p. 166.
[76] *The House of Satan,* p. 61.
[77] *Art of the Night,* p. 17.

NUISANCE: Shakespeare occasionally injected clowning to relieve emotional tension. This does not alter the fact that serious and profound critical ideas warrant serious and profound expression.

NATHAN: It is an outstanding mark of the democratic man that he puts trust in and believes not serious and profound ideas but rather hollow and superficial ideas seriously and profoundly expressed.[78] It is a [further] distinguishing characteristic of the American that he distrusts wit as he distrusts a female 'cello player or a too jovial physician. Instead of discerning in and behind it a mind that, having mastered all the platitudes and grown properly skeptical of most of them, indulges itself in a searching and prophylactic criticism in terms of irony, he appraises wit as being merely the refuge of a none too profound intelligence and its entrepreneur, at best, as something of a clown.[79]

NUISANCE: By clowning you lay yourself open to the charge of being a clown. By writing flippantly you convey the impression that you do not take the theatre seriously.

[78] *Land of the Pilgrims' Pride*, p. 247.
[79] *Ibid.*, p. 246.

NATHAN: It is not that the critic who writes lightly does not take his subject seriously; it is simply that, like a man with the woman he truly and deeply loves, his very seriousness makes him light-hearted, happy and gay. Beauty makes idiots sad as it makes wise men merry. . . . But because the rank and file of critics believe that there is something wrong with the kind of critic who, understanding thoroughly a thing that they themselves do not so thoroughly understand, takes that thing with a pleasantly careless whistle and the jaunty, sauntering swing of a cane, the latter is looked on with disfavor, and favor bestowed instead upon the kind of critic who would wear a long face at a ladies' day in a coon Turkish Bath.[80]

NUISANCE: Then you were only being frivolous when you wrote that "frivolity is often the successful refuge of talents that are incapable of higher flights."

NATHAN (*groaning*): I never write a serious thing that some profound idiot does not arise and say that I don't mean it.[81]

[80] *The Autobiography of an Attitude*, p. 157. Nathan liked this so well that he used it again, word for word, the following year in describing A. B. Walkley in *The House of Satan*, pp. 81–82. The only change was the substitution of Walkley's name for "the latter" in the last sentence here quoted.

[81] *The World in Falseface*, p. 19.

KERNEL OF THE CREDO.—By way of summarizing these summaries, we find that in the art of criticism, as in the art of drama, Nathan recognizes only the most obvious rules. He prefers to regard every critical work as an entity, free from formula. It does not follow, however, that he recognizes no standard of criticism, for he tells us time and again that he judges each play by the very finest example of its type in the entire field. Passing fancies and comparisons carry little weight. In fact, production itself carries little weight; the play is the important thing. Actor-ridden criticism Nathan deplores.

The art of criticism, he contends further, is cold. It avoids indignation, enthusiasm, and sentimentality. It is personal. And very often it is destructive. He holds no brief for what some reviewers refer to as constructive criticism. Nor does he put a premium on consistency. Rather, he upholds the inconsistent critic. And he practises as well as preaches critical honesty and courage.

Such is the art of criticism, as Nathan sees it, and such is the equally important criticism of criticism.

CHAPTER FOUR

Nathan's Influence

NATHAN has told us explicitly and repeatedly that his purpose in writing dramatic criticism has been to serve not drama but his own whims; to reform nothing; to convince no one, himself included. And looking about him in 1917, after twelve years at the job, he had every reason to believe that he had succeeded. The popular glory of Augustus Thomas and David Belasco was undimmed by Nathan's mud-balls, and apparently he had not "disturbed in the least the prosperous mediocrity of our theatre." [1]

In fact, it was the uselessness of dramatic criticism which first attracted him. He tells us that in his nonage he asked himself, "What is the pleasantest and most useless thing to which you may devote your life?" His subsequent deliberation brought only one answer, and eighteen years after he had taken his own advice he still

[1] *Mr. George Jean Nathan Presents*, p. 145.

was able to dedicate these eloquent lines to the uselessness of dramatic criticism:

> For centuries men have written criticism of the
> drama in an effort to improve it, and with it the
> public taste. What has been the result? The *Frogs*
> of Aristophanes, written 405 years before Christ,
> has never been bettered in any way for dramatic
> satire; the *Iphigenia* of Euripides, written 425
> years before Christ, in any way for profoundly
> moving drama; or the *Oedipus Rex* of Sophocles,
> written 440 years before Christ, in any way for
> stirring melodrama. The imperishable drama of
> Shakespeare fingers its nose at all the dramatic
> criticism written before its time, or since. And in
> the matter of improved public taste the most
> widely successful play in the civilized world in
> this Year of Our Lord 1923 is a crook mystery
> melodrama by Avery Hopwood and Mary Roberts
> Rinehart called *The Bat*.[2]

So Nathan says his say without delusions. This play
and that fall short of his personal demands, and he pub-
lishes the fact. If that constitutes public service, very
well. To him it constitutes self-expression, which in turn
constitutes one phase of hedonism, and he is a hedonist.

[2] *The World in Falseface*, pp. 11–12.

Perhaps he does write solely to amuse himself. Perhaps he does write, like Huneker, for "a single hypothetical reader." Nathan himself has said, "The crowd in front of my tent has never been a large one." [3] Yet it is fair to conclude from the large number of his books and from the huge circulations of the newspapers and magazines that have carried his weekly and monthly articles that he has been widely read—possibly the most widely read of living dramatic critics.

Again he delays us by pointing out, "I have never for a moment flattered myself that more than one-fiftieth of my readers in such publications agreed with me . . ." [4] Having felt strongly moved to take issue with a few of his utterances, we readily understand his point. But these occasional differences in no way detract from our hearty respect for and personal agreement with the great body of his critical opinions. Believer or unbeliever, a Nathan reader feels the sway of his charm and logic, his keen insight and his horse-sense. Could any reasonable person read him with some degree of consistency and fail to cast a skeptical glance on sentimentality and pomposity; fail to regard rank indignation with amusement mingled perhaps with scorn; fail to see the theatre as a house of pleasure—the pleasure of genuine enjoyment in superior entertainment, whatever its type?

[3] *The Autobiography of an Attitude*, p. 154.
[4] *Loc. cit.*

Regardless of his intentions and despite his early disappointment at his failure to dethrone Thomas, Belasco and the like, Nathan has an enviable list of achievements. In time he succeeded in alienating at least a part of the theatregoing public from its former favorites, the aforesaid Thomas and Belasco, Eugene Walter, Edward Sheldon, Charles Klein, Owen Davis and George Broadhurst. In addition, he has discovered or has been among the first to lend impetus to the reception of such widely different dramatists as Eugene O'Neill, Sean O'Casey, the earlier Paul Vincent Carroll and William Saroyan, and to such producers as Ziegfeld and the beginning Arthur Hopkins. He has encouraged the Little Theatre movement, has attacked Puritanism and academicism, has ridiculed provincialism, and induced America to accept the best drama of modern Europe.

Today we take all this for granted. And that in itself is a tribute to Nathan's thoroughness. When he became a critic in 1905, and for a dozen years thereafter, he found American drama, almost without exception, stupid, cheap, and hollow. He wrote in 1917:

> The stupidity of the native professional stage has attained to a splendor so grand and unmistakable that one opens one's mouth in dazzled awe before the very majesty of the thing. . . .

It takes brains to be so stupid as this. . . . The thing calls for experience, for training . . .[5]

But only a year later he observed that the old frauds were losing ground, that new and better playwrights and producers were appearing. Progress was slow. In 1922 he described the improved American dramatic taste as "still in the playing-blocks and tin choo-choo-car stage," [6] and again assailed American playwrights who listened only to the clinking dollars, and American newspapers that judged the quality of a play by the size of the producers' advertisement.

By 1931 the picture was vastly different, but he still stood by, rapier in hand, to prick the bubbles of self-complacency:

That the American drama has thus made big strides in the last ten or fifteen years surely no one will deny. That, however, is not the immediate point. The point is that many of our commentators have become so excited over the strides that they have lost all sense of judgment and values and, like youngsters at a circus parade, so deliriously throw their hats into the air during the passing of the bespangled goats and asses that

[5] *Mr. George Jean Nathan Presents*, p. 303.

[6] Stearns, Harold E., ed., *Civilization in the United States; An Inquiry by Thirty Americans* (New York, 1922), p. 247.

they have no strength left when the elephants go by. Among the playwrights who are presently being anointed as men of rare talent we find any number who are little more than Kleins and Thomases in 1931 clothes. . . .

As examples of those who are currently being eulogized out of all proportion to their actual worth we have such as the Messrs. George Kelly, Philip Barry, Paul Green and Sidney Howard.[7]

Nevertheless, as he pointed out, the drama *had* improved. Where Klein, Broadhurst, Thomas, Davis, Walter and Belasco had reigned a decade or two before, now sat O'Neill, Sherwood, Kaufman, Behrman, Anderson, and such. Honesty, courage, and enterprise had replaced triviality, sham, and sentimentality. Now the old hokum died a-borning. Irony and satire appeared. Dramatic "suspense" dwindled in importance. Audiences that remained in the legitimate theatre after the call of the motion pictures were quick to recognize and applaud genuine merit. *Mourning Becomes Electra, Strange Interlude,* and *Winterset* were rewarded with some of the prosperity that previously had gone entirely to *Abie's Irish Rose, White Cargo,* and *Polly Preferred.*

In 1938 Nathan maintained that the American theatre

"has suddenly become recognized as being the most promisingly vital of the world's playhouses." [8] The Russian theatre, superior in organization, has produced not a single new first-rate play in recent years, he pointed out. The Swedish theatre, modeled somewhat after the Russian, relies on importations and revivals. The English theatre is tired, its leading dramatists "dead or played out." The Irish theatre—and Nathan's devotion to Irish drama needs no mention—is dimmed by internal dissension. The German theatre, as he phrases it, "went completely into the discard with the advent of the Nazi aesthetic." [9] The Italian theatre, despite Mussolini's encouragement as patron and playwright, remains backward. The Spanish theatre is "a corpse." And of the French theatre—"the less said the politer." [10]

With its increased importance American drama has assumed increased responsibility, even vaster now that much of continental Europe lies in bondage. And American playwrights are beginning to stagger under the load. The quality of plays declined sharply during the 1941–42 season. But Nathan is here, lashing out and laying on. It is the playwrights, he tells us, who are singly and solely to blame. They dash off plays about the latest news-

---

[8] *The Morning After the First Night*, p. iii.
[9] *Ibid.*, p. v.
[10] *Ibid.*, p. vi.

paper headline. They write with an eye to easy money. They (he excepts O'Neill, Sherwood, Behrman, Hellman, Anderson, and Saroyan) "have utterly no pride in the theatre." Nathan names names: Elmer Rice has become a mere dramatist of popular hot-collars; George S. Kaufman's and Edna Ferber's recent collaborations have been "shameless wooings of the box-office"; Clifford Odets tries cheaply to shock his audiences "into a surprised hospitality"—and so on. Thus Nathan protects his theatre. With witty cruelty he beats off anyone who might bring it harm—anyone, in fact, who does not actually seek its betterment—for he is tremendously ambitious for the American theatre. It is only his purpose, he tells us paraphrastically, "if the theatre be right to keep it right and if wrong to try to set it right. But right or wrong, the theatre!" [11]

To say that the improvements of the last two or three decades have come about solely through the efforts of George Jean Nathan would, of course, be absurd. But that Nathan has been an influence in the revitalization of the American theatre is undeniable. It would be difficult, if not impossible, to find an American dramatic critic of Nathan's time or any previous time who has been less taken in by fads and frauds and charlatanism; who has blasted ignorance and prejudice so consistently, and reined in premature enthusiasms with the

[11] *Ibid.*, p. ix.

cool, strong hand of intelligence; who, for all his "high and mighty sniffishness," as Mencken called it, has been quicker to recognize, more eager to hail genuine talent whenever and wherever it ventured an appearance; and who has held so immutably to the very highest standards —until eventually the playwrights, the producers, and the American public heard and listened. And American drama improved.

Courage and vigor seem to be the keynotes of the new American drama, and in the final analysis it may be found that much of this courage, much of this vigor have stemmed from the incorruptible courage and the inexhaustible vigor of George Jean Nathan.

Nathan has made mistakes. But time has supported most of his findings, perhaps because time—the fads of the moment and the plays of the season—have influenced him so slightly in the application of his measuring stick: the best examples of that particular type of play in all dramatic history. Today, when the earlier published opinions of many critics cause them acute embarrassment, Nathan's earliest books bear rereading for content as well as for style. If anything, they are less readable now because he was often thoroughly right. Many of his startling statements of the teens and twenties seem platitudes today, for their truth is obvious and long accepted. His success story might be entitled "From Heresy to Axiom in Fifteen Years."

When we think of Nathan we are apt to think of his annihilating wit; of his much admired and widely quoted characterization of James M. Barrie as "the triumph of sugar over diabetes"; [12] of his suggestion that Augustus Thomas' *Indian Summer* would be far more intelligent and even somewhat coherent and logical if played "hind end foremost" [13]—a prick to his pomposity from which Thomas, erstwhile dean of American drama, never fully recovered; of the delightful chapter in *Mr. George Jean Nathan Presents* called "Legend's End," which describes in detail the innumerable Belasco hoaxes—the string-pulling and parlor magic and assorted counterfeits—a gala exposé that did, indeed, mark the beginning of the legend's end. Others have fallen before the razor edge of Nathan's ridicule: Maeterlinck, "the Belgian Belasco"; the "Little Red Writing Hoods"; and, as we have noted, the Kleins, the Davises and the Broadhursts of earlier days. The conventional flippancy of Noel Coward has not escaped Nathan's contempt, and although "stagewright" Coward has survived, his status is less exalted since Nathan, in 1935, devoted eleven pages to listing the low comedy and vaudeville sources from which Coward lifted dozens of his gags.

These are only a few of the "countless preliminary

[12] *Comedians All*, p. 169.
[13] *Another Book on the Theatre*, p. 163.

body blows of muscular criticism guided by a muscular mind" [14] with which Nathan has helped to whip American drama into shape. Randolph Bartlett dubbed him "exterminator of humbugs." His wit has blasted parroting playwrights for more than thirty years, exposed their tricks and enumerated their repetitions, that even the casual playgoer might recognize and scoff. His utter disregard for big names and box-office success has bolstered the independence of other critics. If a comic twist would make his point more memorable, he was witty. If cruelty seemed necessary, he was cruel. Often he was both. And he got results.

From his earliest experience as play reviewer on a typically money-minded New York newspaper have sprung innumerable articles challenging the critical value of journalistic reviews. And the subsequent vast improvement in these journalistic reviews during the last two decades already has been noted.

Singlehanded for eight years and still the leader after others joined the fight, Nathan attacked the pompous theorizing of the academicians of drama: Maeterlinck, Brieux, and such on the creative end of the job; William Winter, Richard Burton, Clayton Hamilton, and Brander Matthews on the critical. Says Mencken, "No critic in America, and none in England save perhaps Walkley,

[14] *The Critic and the Drama*, p. 10.

143

has combated this movement more vigorously than Nathan." [15]

The combat was a combined attack against academicism and Puritanism. And since commercial Puritanism frequently was forced upon other critics by their publishers, who were ruled by their prudish and narrow-minded readers, Nathan's crusade against Puritanism was directed against all three. "Vulgarity is itself an art," [16] he argued, upholding the artist against the moralist. Later he added, "A trace of brusque vulgarity is essential to first-rate drama, since drama is, in the Latin sense, primarily a vulgar art. Shakespeare is often as vulgar as Mr. A. E. Thomas is habitually refined." [17] Nathan promptly was condemned as immoral—as immoral, indeed, as the "pornography and smut" of the plays he upheld—plays by such degenerates as Ibsen, Strindberg, Shaw, Andreyev and Gorki. Unabashed, Nathan continued his attacks against the "corsetted emotion" of "mincing, wasp-waisted and furtive" drama. That his arguments eventually carried weight need not be pointed out to any present-day theatregoer.

Nathan's excoriations and castigations have been thorns in the paths of dozens of inferior playwrights, but

[15] Mencken, *Prejudices: First Series*, p. 219.
[16] *Mr. George Jean Nathan Presents*, p. 64.
[17] *Materia Critica*, p. 191.

the debunker de luxe of American drama has not rested on these negative achievements. He has discovered new and better playwrights, recognized and encouraged them, educated the public to appreciate their merits, and so has become the foster father of the new American drama.

Nathan's greatest American find to date is, of course, Eugene O'Neill. During their *Smart Set* days, as we noted, Nathan and Mencken introduced or gave early encouragement to O'Neill, Dunsany, Dreiser, James Stephens, James Joyce, Aldous Huxley, Ruth Suckow, F. Scott Fitzgerald, Willa Cather, Ben Hecht, Sinclair Lewis, and countless others. Another of Nathan's earliest contributions was his recognition of the better Irish dramatists—Synge, Yeats, O'Casey, et al. Still another was his early hearty support of such Europeans as Hauptmann, Wedekind, Shaw and Tchekov, of whom the theatregoers of those days were totally ignorant or flatly disapproving.

Experimental producers have found Nathan sympathetic. He was also the first critic to proclaim in the public prints the artistic achievements of the late Florenz Ziegfeld, and at the same time he championed with equal eloquence the revolutionary productions of Arthur Hopkins. He was among the first to recommend the Kammerny and Moscow Art theatres. He encouraged the Washington Square Players, the Provincetown Players, and other similar groups.

Then there was George M. Cohan. Nathan tells this story in one of his later books:

> I recall that when, in the far days of my critical
> novitiate, I somehow . . . managed to discover
> a considerable virtue in Cohan and, to the disgust
> of my punditical editor, put it into print, I was
> put down . . . as even more vulgar, more illiter-
> ate and more cocky than Cohan himself, and was
> thenceforth denied a bowing privilege to all the
> eminentos of the craft, from William Winter and
> J. Ranken Towse on the one hand to Alan Dale
> and Acton Davies on the other.[18]

Today no one denies the influence which George Cohan exercised on much of the humorous American drama. Again time vindicated Nathan.

And in the last few years he has helped in the launch-ing of other developing young American playwrights, John Steinbeck, Robert Turney, William Saroyan, et al.

But Saroyan, Cohan, Steinbeck, Carroll, O'Neill, Hop-kins, Hecht—all these men and others who have basked in Nathan's approbation—have been blistered by his cen-sure. No blind admirer, no fainthearted fellow afraid of appearing to reverse his own previous judgment, he never

[18] *The Theatre of the Moment*, pp. 251–52.

hesitates to expose a deficiency. And his plaudits are valued even more highly in consequence.

Of all Nathan's discoveries as a critic, none has been happier in results than his early recognition of O'Neill. O'Neill sent three fo'c'sle plays—*The Long Voyage Home, Ile,* and *The Moon of the Caribbees*—to the *Smart Set.* Nathan promptly accepted them for publication, and the friendship began. The two started a correspondence, and soon O'Neill was sending each new play to Nathan for criticism.

Nathan has served O'Neill in more than an advisory capacity. It was Nathan who, as Vladimar Kozlenko put it, "was cleaning . . . the theatrical stalls of dramatic manure" while O'Neill was writing playlets for amateur actors. It was Nathan who cleared the way for O'Neill "by allowing his individuality to shine theatrically unimpaired and by annihilating the previous points of view which criticism had ready for such a dramatist." [19]

It was Nathan, furthermore, who sent the script of O'Neill's first long play, *Beyond the Horizon,* to John D. Williams, who accepted and produced it. The play won the Pulitzer Prize for 1920, and O'Neill was well started. It was Nathan who, admiring *Anna Christie* in

[19] Kozlenko, Vladimar, *The Quintessence of Nathanism* (New York, 1930), p. 16.

script, sent it first to Edgar Selwyn, who read it and turned it down, and then to Arthur Hopkins, who produced it so successfully. And it was at Nathan's urging that O'Neill wrote *All God's Chillun Got Wings* for *The American Mercury*. And there was more and is more . . .

Meanwhile Nathan in his early critical articles was hailing O'Neill as the only American playwright "whose shoulders begin to lift clearly above the local crowd . . . the one writer for the native stage who gives promise of achieving a sound position for himself." Nor did Nathan's initial enthusiasm over this first important American playwright run away with his judgment.

> . . . by sound position I mean a position, if not with the first dramatists of present-day [1921] Europe, at least with the best of the others. . . . O'Neill may, as the theatrical phrase has it, top his writings from year to year. If he does, his future is the most brilliant future that an American playwright has thus far known. And if he does not, his present is already the most brilliant present that any American playwright has thus far known. For O'Neill has an aloof dignity that no other native playwright of his day has; he has a sense of world theme, a sense of character, and he knows how to write. His weakness is the weak-

148

ness of italics and of monotony. He sees life too often as drama. The great dramatist is the dramatist who sees drama as life.[20]

Some of Nathan's comments were less complimentary, but they too served their purpose. O'Neill acknowledged the service in a letter written to Nathan from Provincetown in 1920. "Your criticism of me and mine in the magazine," O'Neill wrote with gusto, "is sure invigorating—grateful as keen salt breeze after much hot air puffing from all sides. If my sublime head were bumping the stars askew, your acid test would sure put a blister of truth on my heinie that would disturb any squatting at ease on the softest complacency." And O'Neill, then thirty-two, added, "God stiffen it, I am young yet and I mean to grow!" [21]

More often, however, in these early days Nathan was fighting to achieve recognition for this man who hated —even as much as Nathan hated it—the cheapness and falseness and trickery of American drama, the man who "alone and single-handed waded through the dismal swamplands of American drama . . . and bore out of them the waterlily that no American had found there before him." [22]

[20] *The Theatre, the Drama, the Girls*, pp. 67–69.
[21] Goldberg, *The Theatre of George Jean Nathan*, p. 149.
[22] *The Intimate Notebooks of George Jean Nathan*, p. 189.

149

And when O'Neill appeared to falter, when two or three of his poorer plays were produced in close succession, when other playwrights and other critics sniggered and pointed their fingers at O'Neill's feet of clay, Nathan stood up and proclaimed, "The truth about O'Neill is that he is the only American playwright who has what may be called size. There is something relatively distinguished about even his failures; they sink not trivially but with a certain air of majesty, like a great ship, its flags flying, full of holes. He has no cheapness, even in his worst plays." Nathan chose that moment, too, to elaborate on O'Neill's contributions. "What O'Neill has brought to the American drama, aside from his own contributions to it, is almost . . . precisely what Shaw brought to criticism of the drama: a gift of independence and courage to others. He has shown the aspiring American playwright that there is a place here for a whole-hearted integrity in dramatic writing, and that there is a public here that is generous in its response to it. He has shown this by patient and often despairing labor . . ." [23]

And now, in 1942, when many of our playwrights show no signs of growth and others are deteriorating, Nathan calls again for O'Neill, whose work "shows a steady inner progress and a greatly increased depth . . . as will be amply proved when his monumental cycle of nine

[23] *Testament of a Critic,* pp. 98–99.

plays known generally as *A Tale of Possessors Self-Dispossessed* is produced." [24] O'Neill also has completed two plays outside the cycle, *The Iceman Cometh* and *Long Day's Journey into Night*. Nathan predicts that when *The Iceman Cometh* ultimately is produced, it will win the Critics' Circle award as the best play of its year. Now, with the majority of our playwrights turned into rabble-rousers, O'Neill alone has not descended from his ivory tower. But O'Neill, Nathan adds, is doing the American theatre a serious disservice "by failing to give it, in its hour of greatest aesthetic need, those fine, aloof plays which he has completed in the unholy dramatic din about him and which yet thoughtlessly he insists upon keeping from the stage." [25]

George Jean Nathan wrote, and Saroyan echoed in 1929, that Nathan takes nothing very seriously. A steady reader would take exception. The alleged harlequin of American criticism discusses O'Neill in utter seriousness, and once in a while he even becomes a bit serious about Saroyan himself.

Nathan's first contact with the former Postal Telegraph messenger boy came in 1933, when the critic was helping to edit *The American Spectator*. Every day for four months the morning's mail contained a manuscript from

[24] *The Entertainment of a Nation*, pp. 4–5.
[25] *Ibid.*, p. 31.

one William Saroyan, hastily typed—single-spaced—on yellow paper. And every one of those manuscripts, whether article, essay, or short story, was accompanied by a lengthy letter. After examining the material, Nathan wrote to Saroyan, "We can't use the articles, essays and short stories but we will take pleasure in accepting for publication the letters." Saroyan wrote back, "Fine! Only the rate for the letters is two cents a word more." The following year *Story* magazine accepted Saroyan's short story, *The Daring Young Man on the Flying Trapeze*, and so the dispute arises as to who may claim the "discovery" of Saroyan, who had discovered his own genius years before and has been proclaiming it loudly ever since.

Actually, Nathan does not claim to have discovered Saroyan or anyone else. That much-abused word is one in which he never indulges. He prefers, rather, to label his contribution "encouragement." His claim to Saroyan is simply that he has read and still reads all of Saroyan's scripts; that he secured productions for *The Time of Your Life, Love's Old Sweet Song*, and *Hello Out There*; and that he has offered Saroyan various morsels of advice, much of which, alas, has been ignored. This sort of advice:

> After reading Saroyan's *The Time of Your Life*, I printed an article, boosting it, fully seven months

before its production. . . . I told Saroyan to throw his *The Hero of the World* and *Story of a Soldier* into the wastebasket; he didn't do it and tried them out in the summer theatres; they are in the wastebasket now. . . .[26]

Nathan, in turn, is indebted to Saroyan for providing live and comment-inciting copy. As Nathan puts it, "Saroyan is the most spectacular item to have invaded the theatre in some years, and the theatre, though it may not have realized it, was itching for just such a phenomenon." [27]

At the Critics' Circle award dinner honoring Saroyan for *The Time of Your Life,* Nathan was allotted two minutes of radio time in which to disprove the widely held theory that Saroyan is crazy. "About eight months ago," Nathan said, "he wrote me he had been offered a substantial advance to write a play for the Lunts and that he was going to work on it at once. He then inquired in the very next sentence who the Lunts were. So maybe these two minutes after all aren't going to be nearly enough." Nathan went on to say that he had long-distance telephoned Saroyan in California several days before, urging him to come to New York to talk at the dinner. "I'd certainly surely love to," Saroyan answered, "and I'd certainly surely do it, but I *can't talk.*" Then

[26] *The Entertainment of a Nation,* pp. 175–76.
[27] "Saroyan Among the Philistines," *Liberty* (Oct. 4, 1941), 24.

he elaborated on his inability to talk and on the outlines of his next five plays, and Nathan's telephone bill for the call was $73.

"If Saroyan is crazy," Nathan managed to continue cheerfully, "his peculiar form of insanity has succeeded in making him the most important newcomer into the American theatre." Since April 13, 1939, when a Saroyan creation first came across the footlights, the American-born Armenian has been the most talked-of personality in the theatre. That first short play, *My Heart's in the Highlands*, was followed soon after by *The Time of Your Life*. After its favorable reception,[28] the inexhaustible Saroyan poured forth in rapid succession *Love's Old Sweet Song* and *The Beautiful People*, not to mention his summer theatre pieces, *Sweeney in the Trees*, *The Hero of the World*, and *Story of a Soldier*; his western production of *Across the Board on Tomorrow Morning*; his New York ballet called *The Great American Goof*; several published books of plays, stories, and essays; and several hundred newspaper and magazine articles and radio scripts—all this between 1939 and 1941. And more recently he has added four new full-length plays and six short plays to the list.

Such squirrelish activity has not deceived the sea-

[28] When the money began to roll in from *The Time of Your Life*, Nathan asked Saroyan what he was going to do with it. "The first thing I do is build the family a big house," he answered. "The kids are growing up and they'll soon be adults and they can't go on all sleeping in the same room."

soned critic. Nathan is much amused by this "off-stage Fregoli," whom he sees hopping behind a screen five or six times and reappearing in unbelievably short order with half a dozen new plays, stories, essays, ballets, and what not—all of them essentially very much alike. "For it is not hard to discern," Nathan points out, "that, whatever form he is occupied with, his technique usually consists in laying hold of a violently eccentric assortment of human fowl and sentimentally attempting to rationalize them." [29] In many cases the result is marred by impatient writing and a woeful lack of organization and careful dramatic planning. "It gives the impression of something quickly done under a momentary inspiration and tossed out of the nest before it is ready to fly; but all the same it often has in it a fertile invention and a curious life nonexistent in many a play meditated and edited fifty-fold." [30]

The surprising thing is that so much of this work dashed off in fire-horse frenzy has genuine merit. *My Heart's in the Highlands* rated Nathan's vote as the best play of 1938–39, despite the fact that Saroyan knew nothing about playwriting when he wrote it. *The Time of Your Life*, as already noted, won Nathan's vote and the general Critics' Circle award for 1939–40. And the

[29] "Saroyan: Whirling Dervish of Fresno," *The American Mercury*, LI (Nov., 1940), 303.
[30] *Ibid.*, p. 305.

Nathan-*Mercury* award for the best play of 1940–41 went to Saroyan's *The Beautiful People*, with the comment, "This is not to record it as an authentically first-rate play or, for that matter, even first-rate Saroyan. But, whatever it was, it was appreciably superior to any other new American play produced during the period in question. More than any other play, it offered evidence of originality, imagination, poetic inspiration and fecund humor, and more than any other it met the demands of a dramatic criticism with standards higher than journalistic reviewing." [81]

Incidentally, the Critics' Circle by a majority vote strangely preferred Lillian Hellman's *Watch on the Rhine*, but invited Saroyan to the annual award dinner to receive second substantial honors. Nathan reports that the Armenian put his arm affectionately around Miss Hellman, whom he had met only once before, and told her she deserved to win the award and that he was delighted she did. The trouble with her plays, he said, however, was that they contained no songs. And for the next hour he sang lustily every song from his plays, demonstrating the type of ditties which he allowed positively would improve her dramas no end. [82]

[81] "Laurels and Raspberries," *The American Mercury*, LIII (July, 1941), 104.

[82] When Nathan introduced him to Clare Boothe, Saroyan burst out with, "What the hell does a beautiful woman like you want to write plays for?"

Of course Saroyan is peculiar, Nathan admits. And in many instances Saroyan's tact and judgment are questionable. But these are reflections upon his momentary intelligence and his lack of experience, not upon his sanity and his ability. Well then, is Saroyan a genius? No, says Nathan. "But he has a fine and original talent and it is only natural, relative youth that he is, that he should grandly mistake it for genius. . . . The trouble with him is simply that when he expresses a thought, whether intelligent or unintelligent, he is firmly convinced that he is the first man to be on deck with it, like a youngster who with his first girl discovers the only true meaning of love." [33] There was, for example, the bare stage idea. "I've got a great new theatrical idea!" he wrote Nathan in high excitement. "Why should there be scenery on a stage? A bare stage is enough in its own possible illusion. It can represent anything to the imagination. I think I've got something there!" Nathan wrote back that the bare stage idea was centuries old, that it went back to the very beginnings of the drama. "Well, anyway," replied Saroyan. And six days later Nathan received the script.

Despite his personal peculiarities and his technical deficiencies, Saroyan has given us several plays that are rich in beautiful feeling and beautiful humor. As Nathan put it, "A badly cut diamond remains nevertheless always

[33] *The Entertainment of a Nation*, pp. 48–49.

more precious than a perfectly cut rhinestone." And he concludes:

> In this William Saroyan, crazy or not crazy, the national theatre, I believe, has discovered its most genuinely gifted new writer. His plays singly and in combination have disclosed . . . a talent which, as yet undisciplined, vainglorious, cock-eyed and pigheaded, is nevertheless the liveliest and most bouncing that has come the way of the local stage in some equinoxes. In that talent, which still resembles a fountain contending against a strong headwind and helplessly splashing itself all over the place, we engage a whimsical imagination, a lenitive sentiment, a fertile humor and a human wonder and ache uncommon to our drama and which in sum make his plays, whatever their occasional critical subordinacies, such welcome additions to the file of American playwriting.
>
> He is a peculiar mixture, this young Saroyan. . . . Although as unabashedly sentimental at heart as . . . an old-fashioned valentine, he has the dramatic gift of making his emotional syrups not only palatable to the most realistically minded auditor but immensely moving. Although his dramaturgy is sometimes as sketchy as a child's

drawing of . . . a moo-moo, he not only gets the effect more usually contrived by the more precise artisan but here and there achieves it with a doubled power. And although he seems superficially to sustain his characters, orchid-like, on the thinnest of thin air, they come to us at the end rounded, whole, and completely intelligible. He writes much too hurriedly and impatiently, a symptom of his brash overconfidence. And his plays, accordingly, are not fully what care and meditation might make them. But I, for one, would rather have them in all their relative crudity than any ten dozen others sedulously polished, like old pairs of cheap shoes, into a surface acceptability.[34]

In nearly four decades in the theatre, Nathan has consistently urged freedom from restraint. He has never tried to hog-tie talent. Nor would he squelch this "fountain helplessly splashing all over the place." Rather, he would help direct its abundant power. We can only hope that Saroyan, when he opens his next letter from Nathan and reads the neat script, will feel the patience, the infinite attention to detail, the striving for perfection—in short, the self-restraint—which another talented fellow has brought to his study of the theatre, and from that ex-

[34] *The Entertainment of a Nation*, pp. 53–54.

ample will yield somewhat to the proffered advice of the dean of American critics.

Thus the Great Dissenter not only exterminates humbugs; he proclaims and fosters genuine talent. He sounds the clarion loud and long. And if he happens to sound it alone, his faith in his judgment does not falter. He believes implicitly that "whatever interests me is good" and "whatever does not interest me is not good." For the lesser critic who believes that "whatever is good interests me" and "whatever is not good does not interest me," Nathan has nothing but scorn. Such a critic would never have been the first to cheer a Saroyan or an O'Casey, a Synge or an O'Neill.

In his latest book, *The Entertainment of a Nation*, Nathan is faithful to the principles of Nathanism. Despite the deadly seriousness of the reigning playwrights, who tend more and more to identify drama with prophecy, he remains, as the very title of his book indicates, primarily a hedonist who firmly holds the theatre accountable for its first duty of interesting an intelligent audience. His catholicity of taste, which includes the art of the slapstick and the art of tragedy, still fails to cover country life —"the hen-and-rooster circuit" of drama in the summer —and that now ancient object of his scorn, the motion picture. The integrity of Nathan the man shines through the surface contradictions of his criticism. True, he who has at times found a place in drama for propaganda is driven by the furiously earnest messages of current plays to see it as the chief threat to the stately pleasure-dome of his dreams. But the fault lies not in him, but in the stars whose course across the dramatic heavens he seeks to chart. Let the furiously earnest dramatists explain why they called in one year for peace at any price and in the next for a fight to the finish. Nathan remains true to himself and to his view of good drama as "*anything* which interests an intelligently emotional group of persons . . ."

Here, then, is a man who has championed the best in drama for more than a generation. A man who at times— at the very moment of writing, for example—has seemed almost out of touch with certain contemporary productions because of his insistence on drama whose appeal may be for time unending. Here is a man who knows his subject so thoroughly that, when he sits in the theatre tonight watching a play unfold, he will measure it by the finest example of its type in the entire field. But when he writes of it, he will write in the idiom of his country and his generation. He will write like a showman, perhaps a too clever showman. He will choose to handle it theatrically rather than academically. This man, who has lived for several decades in quarters crowded with books from floor to ceiling, has no patience with mere academicism. Similarly, he has no respect for mere technical perfection. This man, who holds that criticism must be cold, and whose own criticism occasionally is intensely cold, holds that art must have warmth and feeling, and lacking these has nothing. For drama and emotion are synonymous.

This critic, who has sat in the theatre nightly for more years than some of our better playwrights have been alive, has seen every dramaturgical rule successfully violated. He has seen great plays built around trivial themes. He has seen trivial plays built around great themes. He has seen every trick of the theatre tried and retried, frequently under the guise of originality. And now he tells us that rules are shackles; that form is not of vital importance; theme is not of vital importance; originality is more than one should hope for. Treatment is the thing that matters. A treatment that has life and skill and hot imagination. A treatment that stirs audiences and holds them quiet and speechless in the theatre after the curtain has fallen for the last time.

Much of Nathan's work will endure. Or if "endure" is ambiguous, we might borrow Burton Rascoe's term of apt evasion, "relative permanency." Nathan has achieved relative permanency because of his contributions to drama and the theatre, because of his complete readability, and because he has painted a raucous, realistic and keenly observant picture of the American theatre of his day and time.

Gordon Craig, great son of Ellen Terry and prophet of the new theatre, summed up these reasons pointedly when he wrote to Nathan twenty years ago, "You are one of the few events in the modern theatre . . ."

THE BOOKS OF GEORGE JEAN NATHAN

Europe after 8:15 (with H. L. Mencken and Willard Huntington Wright) . New York, 1914.

Another Book on the Theatre. New York, 1915.

Mr. George Jean Nathan Presents. New York, 1917.

Bottoms Up. New York, 1917.

The Popular Theatre. New York, 1918.

A Book Without a Title. New York, 1918.

Comedians All. New York, 1919.

The American Credo (with H. L. Mencken) . New York, 1920.

Heliogabalus (with H. L. Mencken) . New York, 1920.

The Theatre, the Drama, the Girls. New York, 1921.

The Critic and the Drama. New York, 1922.

The World in Falseface. New York, 1923.

Materia Critica. New York, 1924.

The Autobiography of an Attitude. New York, 1925.

The House of Satan. New York, 1926.

The New American Credo. New York, 1927.

Land of the Pilgrims' Pride. New York, 1927.

Art of the Night. New York, 1928.

Monks Are Monks. New York, 1929.

Testament of a Critic. New York, 1931.

The Intimate Notebooks of George Jean Nathan. New York, 1932.

Since Ibsen. New York, 1933.

Passing Judgments. New York, 1935.

BOOKS OF GEORGE JEAN NATHAN

The Theatre of the Moment. New York, 1936.
The Avon Flows (with Shakespeare) . New York, 1937.
The Morning After the First Night. New York, 1938.
Encyclopaedia of the Theatre. New York, 1940.
The Bachelor Life. New York, 1941.
The Entertainment of a Nation. New York, 1942.